# Race, Class &
# the Apartheid State

# Apartheid & Society

Endgame in
South Africa?

ROBIN COHEN
Co-published with Unesco


Race, Class
& the Apartheid State

HAROLD WOLPE
Co-published with OAU and Unesco


A History of Resistance
in Namibia

PETER H. KATJAVIVI
Co-published with OAU and Unesco

# Race, Class & the Apartheid State

## HAROLD WOLPE

*Reader in Sociology*
*University of Essex*

## James Currey
London

## OAU
Inter-African Cultural Fund · Addis Ababa

 Unesco Press
Paris

First Published 1988 by the
United Nations Educational, Scientific
and Cultural Organization
7 Place de Fontenoy, 75700 Paris
and
James Currey Ltd
54b Thornhill Square, Islington, London N1 1BE
and the Organization of African Unity
Addis Ababa

*British Library Cataloguing in Publication Data*

Wolpe, Harold
    Race, class & the apartheid state
    1. Apartheid—Social aspects—
    South Africa
    I. Title
    305.8′968        DT763
    ISBN 0–85255–319–6 (James Currey)
    ISBN 92–3–102510–4 (Unesco)

Trade distribution of edition published by James Currey
to UK exclusively and all other countries by
J.M. Dent & Sons (Distribution) Ltd, Dunhams Lane, Letchworth,
Herts SG6 1LF
and
Third World Publications, 151 Stratford Road, Birmingham B11 1RD
For all other countries outside UK distribution also by Unesco, Paris

*The ideas and opinions expressed in this book are those of the author and
do not necessarily represent the views of UNESCO.*

Typesetting from author's disks by
Opus, Oxford
Printed in Britain

# Contents

## 5
## The Present Conjuncture:
## the Prospects for Change

# Preface

This book was completed in February 1987 during the state of emergency in South Africa which began on the 12th June 1986. An earlier state of emergency (July 1985 to March 1986) not only failed to stem the popular struggles against the apartheid regime, it actually resulted in the deepening and strengthening of community, political and other organizations. The continued, indeed, the growing resistance of the mass democratic movement led to the still harsher measures of the present state of emergency which, however, have also failed to eradicate the extra-parliamentary opposition. This book is dedicated, as a modest contribution, to the heroic struggles of the South African people to abolish the racist and exploitative apartheid system.

I owe a special debt to Elaine Unterhalter who read and commented extensively on a first draft and provided me, at short notice, with information relevant to specific aspects of the analysis. Much of this has been incorporated into the text which was also revised in the light of her comments.

These revisions involved a complex patchwork of insertions and alterations at numerous points in the manuscript which made the typing of them particularly arduous, especially as they were in my near illegible handwriting. My secretary in the Sociology Department of the University of Essex, Mary Girling, typed the revisions with a minimum of fuss and a maximum of intelligence for which I am deeply grateful.

Both Tony Trew and Laurence Harris read and criticised the revised draft. In different ways their comments were extremely penetrating and often difficult to deal with but also very stimulating and helpful. The text has been much improved as a result of the revisions they induced.

In writing this book I have drawn heavily on a number of my own articles published in *Review, The International Journal for the Sociology of Law, Journal of Southern African Studies*, and in the collections edited by M.Fransman and J.Rex and D.Mason respectively. The full references are cited in the bibliography.

# Unesco Preface

This book has been commissioned by Unesco as part of its struggle against apartheid. This struggle increasingly implies the analysis of the nature of apartheid and of South African society. Indeed, South Africa has emerged, not only as a political issue, but as an important social science 'problem'.

The problem which South Africa poses to social scientists is not simply the condemnation of apartheid. There is the whole question of the explanatory efficacy of competing social science theories, for apartheid emerges both at the level of ideology and at the level of state organisation and policy – the racial allocation by the state of political, social and economic roles. Such racist practice is not an epiphenomenon of South African society, neither is it simply the rationalisation of a form of advanced capitalism, nor is it only a form of settler colonialism. Again, it is not sufficient to say that South Africa is a racist society for race, although of central importance, operates there in specific ways and does not eliminate class formation.

Class formations in South Africa articulate with racial divisions and with deliberately fostered ethnic rivalries. The situation is highly complex and though class consciousness is not automatic, yet competition among classes and groups plays an increasingly important role within South African society.

It is not surprising therefore that a number of theoretical positions exist to explain the evolution of apartheid society. Harold Wolpe analyses these positions indicating what, in his opinion, are the insufficiencies of these or their relevance. And he goes beyond this to analyse the forces of resistance to the state apparatuses, forces both institutional, e.g. the United Democratic Front, and grounded in the participatory nature of popular revolt. This book then should be read both as an analysis of the current literature on South Africa and as an explanation of oppression and the struggle against it. While Unesco has sponsored this book, the views expressed are those of the author. They do not commit the Unesco Secretariat.

# Introduction

Despite an impressive and growing literature on the South African political and economic system, analyses, as distinct from descriptive studies, of the state and, more generally, of the political sphere, remain surprisingly underdeveloped. This applies no less to the literature of the period since 1948, when the present regime came to power, than to historical accounts of politics and the state before that date.

The intensification of political conflict, in particular the re-emergence and development, on an unprecedented scale, of mass political opposition which challenges the very existence of the apartheid system, has also posed more sharply than hitherto certain theoretical problems in the analyses of the economic and political conditions of social transformation in South Africa. In the political field, these problems relate to conceptions of the relationship between class and race and between the political structure of apartheid and the capitalist economy as well as of the form of the state and political arena and the structural conditions of political struggles.

The issues involved are not only of theoretical interest but have a direct relevance to the formulation of political perspectives and objectives. For example, a theoretical position which, based on the concepts of race, views apartheid as exclusively a racial order, results in a political perspective (such as black consciousness) which stresses only racial antagonisms and alliances. By contrast, the African National Congress (ANC) and its allies advance the theory of colonialism of a special type, which, based on a conception of linkages between race and class, grounds a political perspective which accords to the black working class a leading role in the overthrow of the apartheid system including the transfer of the 'banks and monopoly industry . . . to the ownership of the people as a whole'. (ANC Speaks, 1977, p.14)

The overall objectives of this book are twofold. The first objective is to examine theoretical formulations which are relevant to alternative political perspectives in contemporary South Africa. There is no intention, however, to systematically present these alternatives. Rather, the purpose is to identify theoretical positions on the relationship between race and class and the nature of the political system, which predominate in the South African literature and to

1

discuss their effects on political perspectives and analysis. The choice of the literature examined in this part of the book has been governed, in part, by its political importance – in the case, for example, of liberal theory and the theory of colonialism of a special type – and in part by its pertinence to one of my main objectives which is to show how, in variant ways, concepts widely employed close off the concrete investigation of issues relevant to political analysis.

The second objective is to indicate how the insights gained from this theoretical critique may be utilised in analysing the concrete conditions of political struggle. In this respect too, no attempt is made to provide a full and systematic analysis of the present conjuncture. Instead, the analysis is aimed at illustrating the importance of properly linking class and race on the one hand and of locating struggles in relation to the structures of the political system on the other.

The theoretical focus of the book, then, is on class and race and the state and the political arena. The argument may be summarised in the following terms.

Conventionally, accounts of South African society have been based on theoretical positions which are either race or class reductionist in the sense that explanations of the social order are assumed to be explicable by either of these phenomena operating in isolation from one another. Only the theory of colonialism of a special type refuses these reductionisms but, because it posits an inevitable and functional relationship between racial domination and capitalism in South Africa it is unable to exploit to the full the conception of the interlinkages between race and class. The thrust of this section of the book will be to argue that race and class and the capitalist economy and the system of white domination stand in a contingent relationship to one another. This opens the way to a consideration of the question of the class content of struggles against white domination.

Before proceeding to summarise briefly the second theoretical argument, it is necessary to clarify in advance the concepts of class and race as they are used in the book. With regard to the former concept, it is only necessary at this stage (there is a further discussion in Chapters 1 and 3), to say that the Marxist notion of classes as defined in terms of relations of production (ownership/non-ownership of the means of production and the expropriation of surplus labour) is used throughout although in, this form, it is merely a starting point for the elaboration of a more concrete conception which is set out in Chapter 3.

The term 'race' is used *strictly* to refer to social categorisations. That is to say, however much biological notions are employed to justify the definition of racial groups in South Africa, those groups are actually constituted by a process of social definition which employs biological terms to define social not biological groups. The social definition of these groups in South Africa is imposed and maintained in all the spheres of the social formation and is embedded in the legal, political, ideological and economic institutional order. Given this conception, no distinction is made between 'race' and 'ethnicity' for the purposes of this book, except where this may be required by the context. In addition, the terms 'apartheid', 'racial domination' and 'white domination' are used interchangeably.

The second major theoretical focus is on the political sphere or system. Little attention has been paid in the South African literature to the structure of the state or to the terrain of politics related to, but outside of, the state apparatuses. In particular, the political terrain is normally analysed only in terms of the content and conduct of struggles and little or no attention is paid to the way in which these struggles are structured by the specific form of that terrain and of the state.

The argument is that, since 1948, the state and the political terrain have undergone major structural transformations and that these transformed structures characterise three different periods. The significance of these structures is that they contribute to the shape of political contestation. Thus, for example, during the 1960s the state was able virtually to obliterate the terrain of extra-parliamentary politics with profound effects on the political alternatives open to the national liberation movement.

The general argument is that an understanding, in any given period, of the political conjuncture requires an analysis which, on the one hand, is historically specific and, on the other hand, is not reduced solely to a descriptive account of struggles and events. To achieve this, it is necessary to analyse not only the prevailing struggles but also the structural conditions which mark the character of a period and provide the specific context against which the content and direction of political conflicts can be understood.

In the first chapter, in order to open up the issues to be discussed, three obstacles to political analysis in the South African context are analysed. In Chapter 2, liberal modernisation theory and the theory of colonialism of a special type are examined and this is followed in Chapter 3 with an attempt to theorise the relationship between race and class. Chapter 4 provides a periodisation of the political system in the period of apartheid. This period is taken to have been inaugurated with the accession to power of the National Party in 1948. Although the regime did not immediately transform all the structures which owed their origin to the previous period of segregation, nonetheless, a process was set in train which created structures which demarcate the era of apartheid from that earlier period. The final chapter examines certain aspects of the present conjuncture and its possible trajectory.

# 1 Analysing the South African Political System: Theoretical Obstacles

Three conceptual obstacles have tended to impede the analysis of the South African political system. These are, first, a particular variant of the idea of the continuity of South African history; second, reductionist views of class and race; and, third, the overwhelming priority given, in the analysis of the state and the political terrain, to the *content* and *conduct* of struggles, with little, if any, attention being paid to the structural conditions and context of such struggles.

It should be made clear that these impediments are not the exclusive property of any single approach but may be found to operate either singly or in combination in analyses of the South African social formation which are informed by different theoretical perspectives. The effect of these obstacles is that significant questions about the character and trajectory of political struggles cannot be posed and investigated.

Thus, for example, the simplistic view of historical continuity which over-emphasises the *continuity* of racial domination and thereby fails to recognise the significance and implications of changes which are less than fundamental, may be found in some (but not in other) liberal, Marxist and black consciousness accounts.

The same applies to the two other conceptual obstacles referred to above. Thus, race reductionism makes it impossible to pose questions about the class content of national struggles and conversely economic reductionist notions of class exclude questions about the national content of class struggles. Finally, the restriction of political analysis to descriptive accounts of conflict without setting these conflicts in their structural setting makes it virtually impossible to understand properly their significance in relation to the process of political transformation.

What follows, therefore, in this chapter is not so much a critical analysis of different theoretical *frameworks* but rather an examination of the effects of particular conceptual obstacles which may be found to be common to some versions of all the theoretical approaches employed in the South African context.

### THE OVER-EMPHASIS OF HISTORICAL CONTINUITY

The central problem with the thesis which over-emphasises the thread of continuity in South African history is that, by imposing a uniformity on that history, it tends to suppress important questions about the nature and conditions of change in the society. This is so because, from this point of view, changes which occur in different periods of history are *assumed* to be superficial in the sense that they leave existing structures and relations essentially unaltered in all important respects. What results from this is a failure to recognise and analyse (i) emerging tensions and contradictions within the social system and (ii) structural transformations of the 'space'in which conflicts are waged, and this, in turn, inhibits an adequate assessment of the significance of those conflicts.

The point may be illustrated by reference to the way in which the period of apartheid is understood in relation to pre-1948 South African history. On the one hand, it is frequently implied that apartheid is simply a new name for a set of structures and relations which, in all fundamental respects, were established some 300 years ago; the history of South Africa is *co-terminus* with the history of apartheid – the latter being merely the modern expression of relations implanted in the past. On the other hand, a similar conclusion is reached by another route. It is widely argued that the National Party, in 1948, inaugurated a new, distinctive phase of South African history. Nevertheless, that distinctiveness is frequently conceived of not as a structural transformation but merely as the intensification, modernisation and rationalisation of the already present structures of white domination. [1] Thus, in this instance too, despite the recognition of a distinctive period, the emphasis remains on continuity at the expense of questions about discontinuity, or, at least questions about the specific significance and explanation of such changes as have occurred.

Consider, for example, the discussions of black education, which has been a crucial sphere of political conflict since the mid-1950s and particularly during the past ten years. The introduction of the Bantu Education Act in 1953, the dramatic increase in the number of Africans in primary schools which followed, the significant rise in African pupils in secondary schools in the recent past, the emergence of the black universities and schools in the late 1960s as centres of resurgence of powerful opposition to the regime – all these, and other changes, are represented, in the continuity thesis under consideration, as nothing more than the reproduction of white domination. Questions such as *why* the act was introduced when it was and how the changing patterns of black education and the emergence of opposition in the schools is to be explained are simply not posed, and cannot be given the assumption that the changes which occurred and are occurring (in education and in other respects) are nothing more than the reproduction of the fundamental structure of the social order. [2]

In its crudest form, this continuity thesis reduces to an untheorised, descriptive account of the racial content of policies, discourses and practices. But a more sophisticated version is also found in the social science literature which argues that the reproduction of the racial order is the outcome of the unchanging and 'pure' racial motivations of dominant actors. These motivations are primordial, simply given in history, and hence neither their presence nor their effect on social action require explanation. Furthermore, since racial motivations are primordial, they are also prior to and autonomous of other social structures or processes (for example, class, the economy). As will be further discussed in Chapter 2, the social structure is seen to be composed of 'plural groups', that is to say, racial or ethnic entities. The hierarchical and unequal relations of these plural groups is the core of the social system and its reproduction is explained in terms of the racial or ethnic motivations of the actors that comprise groups. In this view, which, interestingly enough, is to be found in some liberal, racist and black consciousness literature (although vastly different inferences are drawn) the continuity of racial domination is the expression of invariant, primordial racial motivations. A major problem with this is that due to its single-minded reductionism, it provides no space for the analysis of the complex interplay between, and significance of, the multiple determinants of the social order. Therefore, it is unable to pose, let alone solve, questions about the conditions under which racialised practices come into existence, persist and change; the intersection of ideological, political and economic processes in the shaping of interests and conflicts and the effect of these processes on the alignment and opposition of social forces.

An inadequate notion of continuity also appears in the opposing positions in the debate concerning the relationship between capitalism and racism in South Africa. This will be discussed more fully in Chapter 2 but it is important to refer to this debate here insofar as it touches on the question of continuity.

According to liberal modernisation theory, there is a necessary contradiction between capitalism and racism. Capitalism, particularly in its advanced industrial stage, operates in terms of rational criteria of resource allocation. Racism, (and here, liberal theory usually incorporates, more or less intact, the notion of primordialism referred to above), on the other hand, adopts other, irrational, criteria. There is, thus, an invariant, not a contingent, contradiction between capitalism and racism. That contradiction will persist until one or other triumphs. Since it is known in advance that the relation is one of contradiction, there is no further need to investigate in what way and to what extent this may not be the case.

In most of the South African Marxist literature, [3] particularly through the 1970s, the opposite was argued. It was not only shown that racism was beneficial to the development of South African capitalism, it was also contended that there was a *necessary*, not a contingent, link between capitalism and racism such that the latter could be dismantled only with the demolition of the former. Here, too, since it is known in advance that racism serves capitalism, there is no further need to examine in what way and to what extent this may not be the case.

I will return to this aspect of the debate in Chapter 2 and again in Chapter 4, but here I want to suggest a different approach which avoids the editing out of issues crucial to the analysis of contemporary South Africa. At this stage, it is sufficient to state that the relationship between capitalism and white domination must be seen as an historically contingent, not a necessary one. Moreover, that relationship will be both functional and contradictory at the same time – functional for the reproduction of certain relations and class positions and contradictory for others. The contention is that the formation of structures and relations is always the outcome of struggles between contending groups or classes and that this outcome is Janus-faced, being always simultaneously functional and contradictory. Which pole of the relationship will be dominant depends on the historically specific conditions of the social formation. But that dominance, precisely because of its contingency, is always vulnerable in two ways: firstly, the 'fit' or contradiction between capitalism and racism may be eroded or expanded within particular social and economic spheres and the outcome may be, leaving aside the possibility of the demise of the capitalist social order, a shift towards increased functionality or sharpened contradiction resulting, in either case, in significantly altered conditions of struggle.

It is precisely the analysis of the alteration of the conditions which is of central importance. This is not to suggest that each moment in history is to be treated as uniquely discrete. The point (as will be argued more fully in Chapter 4) is to recognise the significance of diversity and discontinuity within a process of continuity.

The contemporary debate about the reality of the 'reforms' introduced by the Botha regime illustrates, in a very concrete way, the adverse consequences of the failure to make this distinction. A common position in this debate is the contention that all the reforms which the regime claims to have introduced, from the 'real' recognition of black trade unions to the empty tri-cameral parliament, are to be written off as nothing more than as mere measures which reproduce white domination.

This, however, is to confuse the question of the extent to which particular changes are fundamental, with the quite separate, but related, question of the effects of changes, which are less than fundamental, on the terrain of conflict in the society. Here a simple, dichotomous conception of change is at work: either the system is totally transformed or it remains unchanged. This is an old problem which becomes sharply posed when the opposition between revolutionary and reformist strategies and change is defined too rigorously. The difficulty with this approach is that the over-arching structure of white domination is seen to be always perfectly implemented by the policies pursued and unaffected, except by way of 'modernisation, intensification and rationalisation', by changes in policies. Here, a generalised and, so to speak, summary description of the social order functions to obliterate the possibly contradictory effects of change.

A generalised characterisation of the social formation may be indispensable as a starting point of analysis, or, it may be added, acceptable as a shorthand description of South Africa in the ideological discourses of political organisations or as a descriptive term to summarise the overall effects of historically specific processes which have already been analysed. However, a problem arises when shorthand descriptive terms – 'racial domination,' 'capitalism' – become substitutes for that analysis. In this event, the terms become the bases for accounts of South African history which over-emphasise continuity. What is then lost is the analysis of the all-important differences and discontinuities both in the processes through which such domination comes to be constructed and, indeed, the changing forms it assumes. That is to say the descriptive term becomes a substitute for analysis. But this is untenable because 'white domination'/'capitalism' exist only in specific institutional and organisational forms and in specific practices within different social spheres, and the relationship between these, as has already been suggested, is not necessarily harmonious.

The importance of this formulation lies in the fact that it makes clear that, even if the 'overall' product of these concrete organisational and institutional processes can aptly be labelled 'white domination'/ 'capitalism', nonetheless, it is only by refusing to remain at that general level that it is possible to open up a field of investigation which is otherwise obscured. In the first place it allows us to recognise that the apparatuses in and through which white domination is maintained may stand not only in a functional, complementary and supportive relationship to one another, but also in relations of contradiction and conflict. In the second place, the possibility is opened up that, within certain apparatuses and institutions, white domination may continue to be reproduced, albeit in changing forms, while within others it becomes, at the same time, eroded. Conceived of in this way, the notion of continuity becomes problematised: we are led, rather, to investigate the specific, changing, institutional and organisational forms in which the system may be simultaneously transformed and reproduced and also, the uneven, heterogeneous and contradictory processes of that reproduction and transformation. It

9

follows that the implementation of state policies is never merely the reproduction of 'white domination' as such, but rather a change in, perhaps even an erosion of, the specific, concrete and differentiated forms of existence of that domination.

The important analytical (and political) question then is: what concrete effect do these changes – whether reforms or not – have on the structural and conjunctural conditions of political action? This raises the question of structural periodisation which I will address later.

CONCEPTS OF CLASS AND RACE [4]

Theoretical advance and the production of historically specific accounts of the political system have been especially difficult in South Africa due to the overwhelming opacity of the ideological and political structures of racial domination and the empirical obviousness of racial oppression.

In Chapter 2 I will discuss the way in which the political system is theorised in certain contrasting accounts of South African society. At this stage, however, I want only to explore more generally the implications, for the analysis of the political sphere, of the concepts of class and race as these are widely used in South African writing.

The central theoretical question in the analysis of the South African social formation is how the relationship between race and class should be understood. The answer given to this question has a direct bearing, at the political level, on the way in which the struggle against white domination may be characterised. In common with other countries, two currents of political struggle emerged in twentieth century South Africa – nationalism and socialism. What was specific to South Africa, at least by comparison with other African countries, was that, firstly, the black nationalist movement, organised primarily by the African National Congress (founded in 1912) was based on the struggle against white domination which, after 1910, was imposed not by an external colonial power but by the dominant white forces inside the country and secondly, the class struggle for socialism found organised expression in the formation of the South African Communist Party in 1921.

In the ideological and political discourses of nationalism and socialism, as these have been expressed by the political movements in the struggle against the existing system in South Africa, the class struggle and the national struggle have been and still are frequently represented, as quite separate modes of political intervention each with its own distinctive objectives and different social constituencies. Indeed, it is sometimes argued that nationalism and socialism are necessarily opposed. Thus, from a 'populist' standpoint, the national struggle is presented as being in the interests of the entire population, not of a particular class; and from a different perspective the contention is that nationalism is the ideology of the bourgeoisie.

However, a different theory of the South African revolution, in which the *convergence* of the class and the national struggle is stressed, has been developed. As Pallo Jordan (1983) has observed:

> The South African liberation movement headed by the A.N.C. is a multi-class alliance embracing movements that draw their inspiration from two modern political currents, nationalism and socialism ... The complex interaction between these two currents in our movement has been dealt with elsewhere. We shall focus here on how these two grew together, leading first to a political alliance and later to the emergence of a common approach to the immediate tasks facing our people and our country. (p.3)

In this section, the purpose is to examine the theoretical underpinnings of the two positions which represent national and class struggles as necessarily separate and, indeed, opposed to one another. It will be argued that these positions are based, whether implicitly or explicitly, upon accounts of the historical development of, and contemporary situation in, South Africa which rest on unacceptable reductionist theories of race or class or, indeed, on an untheorised combination of both reductionisms which entails a conception of two autonomous spheres – a racial order and a class structure. The examination of the limitations of these approaches will prepare the way for the formulation (in Chaptér 3) of a view of the relationship between political domination and economic exploitation which escapes either reductionism and opens the way to analyses of the contingent relationship between class and national struggles, including their convergence.

It is of interest to note that contentions concerning the autonomy of or the opposition between class and nationalist struggles continue to be held across the political spectrum despite the fact that recent developments in South African capitalism and in the character of political struggles have put in question these contentions and the theories of class and race on which they are based.

The most significant of these changes has been the growth and stabilisation of the black industrial working class which, since the early 1970s, has become increasingly organised in trade unions and increasingly drawn into a range of oppositional political struggles. The effect of this has been to pose more sharply and more immediately than ever before the issues about the role and political objectives of the black working class in the mounting challenge to the regime and social order. In short, the emergence of the organised black working class as the dominant political actor has in practice put into question the radical distinction hitherto often drawn between the class struggle (for socialism) and the national struggle for a national democratic, non-racial state. In turn, this has brought to the fore, more compellingly than in any earlier period, the theoretical question of the relationship between class and race.

More particularly, contemporary changes have helped expose the analytical (and political) limitations which stem from the reductionist conceptions of the social order. One of these limitations is related to the fact that reductionist theories tend to replicate, albeit by a different path, the analytical limitations which flow from the idea of historical continuity which was criticised above; another is that they result in an unsatisfactory view of the political system.

There are, of course, numerous theories of race relations. It is unnecessary to examine these here [5] since my purpose is to focus narrowly on the underlying premises of these theories and, in particular, to indicate briefly their theoretical shortcomings in relation to the analysis of South Africa. In fact, although the remarks which follow are directed more particularly at the theory of plural society which focuses virtually exclusively on the plurality of groups defined in racial or ethnic terms, they also apply to other approaches insofar as plural theory is explicitly or implicitly incorporated into them. For example, in some interpretations of the notion of internal colonialism. [6]

Race-based theories conceive of race (whether regarded as primordial or otherwise given, or as socially constructed) as the irreducible constituent and determinant of social structure and relations. The social structure is then theorised on the basis of individual subjects and groups who owe their formation, their unity and their homogeneity to a single racial origin. Correspondingly, the social relations within and between these groups are asserted to be exclusively governed by racial categories: that is, the interests of racial groups are derived from, and are formulated exclusively in terms of, their racial attributes.

Strictly construed, this leads directly to a conception of the existing social order in which the racial entities which comprise the social structure are analytically treated as if they are internally homogeneous and undifferentiated, at least, in any material respects. Indeed, it is only possible to represent racial entities as homogeneous and unified by a theoretical process in which the racial basis of group formation is abstracted from other bases of differentiation such as property ownership, market position, access to institutions of political power and so forth. It is then assumed that within the racial group there is a uniform, common and equal investment in the racial ordering of the social system. One well-known formulation of this position argues that:

> Social classes in the Marxian sense of the relationships to the means of production exist by definition, as they must in any capitalist country, but they are not meaningful social realities. Clearly, pigmentation, rather than ownership of land or capital is the most significant criterion of status in South Africa. (Van Den Berghe, 1967, p. 267)

The problem with this is that it defines away the central question which requires examination in the South African context – the relationship of class and race. It simply assumes that race operates autonomously, unaffected by other social processes, to produce social inequalities.

It is, however, of considerable political importance to recognise that the formation and maintenance of racial groups take place in specific contexts and are subject to both centrifugal and centripetal pressures. These pressures are, in part, bound up with the fact that in South Africa racial groups were formed, through complex processes, out of categories which occupied vastly different positions in the society and, furthermore, that the internal differentiation of these racial groups has continued uninterruptedly, albeit unevenly. One need only think of the changes in the class structure within racial groups which have occurred over the past 100 years or so. For example, within the African population, de-peasantisation and proletarianisation and the emergence of a petite bourgeoisie, a large stratum of tertiary sector employees and a very small bourgeoisie; within the white population, the enlargement and changing structure and composition of the capitalist class, the decline of small farmers, the growth of agri-business, extensive de-proletarianisation and so forth.

While it is undoubtedly the case that race constituted a vital mechanism in these processess of class formation and transformation and became a common ingredient in the definition of the interests of all the classes within each racial group, it is equally clear that the different positions of each of these classes resulted in changing, different and frequently contradictory demands regarding the need for and content of white domination and the opposition to it. If we generalise these considerations to the social formation as a whole, what this suggests is that the effect of a race reductionist theory is to insulate from enquiry conditions and processes which may be pertinent to the cohesiveness and fragmentation of racial groups and thus to the possibilities of social change.

There is a further problem with racial relations theories and, in particular, the plural theory already referred to. The central concern for race-based theories, of whatever variety, is the existence of structures of racial inequality, that is, of racial stratification which is generated by racially motivated processes. Indeed, the social structure is conceived of as an hierarchical racial order constituted by competing and unequal racially defined groups which are assumed to be internally homogeneous. Thus, while the boundaries of racial entities are established in terms of racial categories, the description of those entities includes also an account of their unequal political, social and economic power, relative to one another.

Now, although conflicts are said to focus on race as such and to take place between racially bound groups over racially defined interests, what this approach has, unwittingly, led to is an identification of classes with racial groups since these groups are differentiated, relative to one another, in terms of their access to wealth and power as well as their status ranking. The racial group becomes a class under a racial or ethnic label. It is curious, therefore, that there should still be an insistence upon the irrelevance of the processes of class formation to the analysis of a plural social order. Yet, this is the case and as a consequence the analysis remains trapped in the narrow confines of race reductionism.

It is, of course, possible that a total overlap between race and class may occur, as is implied by race reductionist theories, and where it does, there seem to be no tenable grounds for excluding class analysis in favour of race reductionism. Nor, as was argued above, do such grounds exist where the racial groups differentially incorporate different classes or class fractions, as in South Africa.

Does it follow, however, that race reductionism must give way to an economic class reductionism? Economic reductionist versions of Marxism, which have had some currency in the South African social science and political literature, lead in this direction.

It is not intended either to review the literature which bears the mark of this reductionism, or, at this stage, to discuss the political positions which have emanated from it. Rather, I want to touch only briefly on this approach insofar as it posits a necessary autonomy of class and race and reduces the explanation of their relationship to the imperatives of the former.

From a Marxist standpoint, the indispensable starting point of an analysis of contemporary South African society is the process of capital accumulation and correspondingly the relations between capital and labour. There is a voluminous literature which argues, in different ways, that such a starting point does not necessarily entail an economic reductionism. I will return to this point in Chapter 3.

In reductionist Marxism, however, class is not merely conceptualised as an economic relation of production, it is also assumed that relation immediately and directly defines the interests of the class entities which are constituted. That is, the classes and the individuals who comprise them owe their formation, their homogeneity and their unity to a single, economic, position. Here, what Marx referred to as 'the class for itself' is collapsed into 'the class in itself' – that is to say, no space is allowed for the contribution of non-economic conditions to the formation of class interests.

It is clear that this approach offers no conceptual basis for an analysis of the specific conditions in which racial categorisations come to provide the content of class struggles and/or the basis of organisation of interests in a manner which both cuts across class divisions and yet may serve to sustain, change (for example, racialisation or deracialisation) or undermine them. Rather, echoing race reductionist theories, it presents an abstract account of class interests – abstract in the sense that these are emptied of the concrete racial categorisations which, in South Africa, are a major means of the internal differentiation of classes. Race here becomes merely an external instrument for the reproduction of class interests which are assumed to be *entirely* defined by the economic relation of production.

Thus, in the pluralist approach, political concerns are defined as if they have no links with the economy; by contrast, reductionist Marxism allows the political only insofar as it reflects economically determined interests. Either way, the political sphere is oversimplified by one or other theoretical closure which not only grounds the contention that the national and class struggles are necessarily separate, but also makes it impossible to analyse the complex intersection of these struggles in the political arena.

STRUCTURE AND CONFLICT: THE TERRAIN OF POLITICS

In the previous section the focus was on the narrow limits imposed by reductionist theories on the definition of political concerns. In this section attention shifts from political *concerns* to a consideration of the *structure* of the political terrain.

The discussion will be conducted through an examination of Nolutshungu (1982), Davis and Bob Fine (1985) and Bob Fine (1984). The reason for concentrating on these texts is that they are among the few works that attempt to deal explicitly with conceptualisation of the political sphere as a terrain of conflict. In *Changing South Africa: Political Considerations* (1982), in an attempt to identify what he calls the 'specifically political' (p.xii), Nolutshungu refers to the idea of the morphology or structure of the political sphere as one crucial means of escaping an economic reductionism while, at the same time, recognising that the political is conditioned by the economic. Although he fails to exploit the potential of this notion, a critique of his exposition makes it possible to take the argument further.

On the other hand, Davis and Bob Fine, through a critical analysis of some accounts of recent South African political history, written from the perspective of the ANC, reject any attempt to define the structural specificity of the political arena and, instead, emphasise the character of political struggles. Theoretically, their work stands on the same terrain as the social history school of which Van Onselen is a leading representative [7] and provides the opportunity to discuss briefly the common limitations of this approach. It will become clear that, like the earlier discussion in this chapter, the points in issue are by no means only academic but have a direct pertinence to political analysis.

Nolutshungu attempts to go beyond a mere critique of economic reductionism by offering an alternative approach which allows political domination and economic exploitation to be grasped simultaneously. He wishes to do this by defining the specificity of the political in South Africa.

He begins with the contention that, hitherto, the analysis of the possibilities of political change have been marred by either a one-sided emphasis on the political, ideological and legal superstructure or, as at present, by an economic reductionism within both Marxist and liberal approaches. The problem, common to both these approaches, despite their other fundamental differences, is that neither offers the theoretical means necessary for an enquiry into the question of *political* change.

In the liberal argument, capitalism (or industrialism) is thought to have a dissolving effect on the archaic and particularistic orientations which govern social action in pre-capitalist or in pre-industrial societies. More especially, the imperatives of the industrial economy are believed to undermine the operation of criteria which rest on ascribed given qualities of actors (for example, those supposedly related to race) and which serve to retard both capitalist production and the development of a rational and democratic legal order. Against this Nolutshungu advances two points. Firstly, he demonstrates the invalidity of the view that capitalism and liberalism are necessarily linked and, secondly, and more importantly, he contends that the effect of the capitalist economy on the polity will depend fundamentally on the nature of the political sphere itself and this is precisely what liberal theory fails to specify:

> Neither identifying capitalist growth with liberalization and democratization nor, even less rejecting that identification, obviates the need within liberal thinking for a specific account of political change. (p.23)

Marxist analyses of South Africa suffer from a similar limitation. In rejecting the liberal contention that South African capitalism '. . . is a liberalizing and progressive force which has been hampered in its work by the external imposition of racial rule and ideology' (ibid, p.4), Marxists have asserted that the economy determines and produces those racial structures and practices which are conducive to its expansion and reproduction. In this view racism is generated within the economy and ' . . . only the economic determination of politics and its economic functions' (p.38) is emphasized. Politics and the state are merely the means to economic ends. Once more, the role of the political, except as a direct reflection of the economy, is de-emphasised and little, if any, importance is accorded to the specific political conflicts which are generated in and structured by the political terrain.

As against these approaches, Nolutshungu is

> . . . mainly concerned to make room for a political discussion of change. (To) seek to identify what is specifically political and to advance a view of politics as not merely instrumental to economic ends, or passively reflecting economic determi-nations, but as itself a distinctive field with relations and concerns, modes of behaviour and values, particular to itself. (p.xii)

However, it is central to Nolutshungu's argument, as against liberal theory, that the political cannot be conceived of in isolation from the economy – ' . . . dominance and exploitation are integrally related' (p.xii). Throughout the text the co-existence and inter-relationship between political domination and economic exploitation is stressed. Indeed, ' . . . political domination is . . . always a condition of the maintenance of exploitive relations' (p.55). The question this leads to is the one which was posed earlier in this chapter: how can the relation between political domination and economic exploitation be conceptualised as integral and yet an economic reductionism avoided?

Nolutshungu bases his answer to this question on the concept of relative autonomy:

> To assert that politics has a practical and important distinctness and relative autonomy is to say that it is not simply determined by other aspects of social life (or levels of social structure); that it has an internal character and dynamic that cannot be deduced or predicted from a description of economic relations, however complete . . . (p.37)

The notion of relative autonomy, however, has to be further specified if it is to operate as more than a gesture and advance this argument. Nolutshungu's contention is that the relative autonomy and distinc-tiveness of the political terrain is established through its specific *concerns* and *structures* such that the struggles in that terrain cannot ' . . . merely represent, with total fidelity, the contending interests of classes economically defined.' (p.64) There are, therefore, two

17

elements to the argument: one centres on the specificity of political concerns, the other on the specificity of the structure of the political.

In general terms, according to Nolutshungu, the concerns of the political system centre on freedom, domination, democracy and not on economic well-being or accummulation. As he expresses it:

> Politics is a distinctive field of action consisting in the relations of domination and subordination, and of freedom and self-government, whether they are expressed in formal organization or in habits or tendencies of alignment and opposition. Every political order is, essentially, a more or less distinctive combination of coercion and 'consent' which defines the provenance of ideology in politics as a distinctive field. (p.60)

The difficulty with this is that by drawing so sharp a distinction between political and economic concerns, an economistic conception of both economy and class is re-introduced. Thus, the concerns of the economy become economic interests which are, apparently, unadulterated by political and ideological ingredients. But struggles over profit and wages levels, over the division of labour and other economic objectives, always entail political ingredients and frequently political ends – that is to say struggles in the economy may involve contestation about democracy and freedom in the society at large as well as about the racialisation or de-racialisation of the division of labour and much else of a 'non-economic' character.

Likewise, it is clear that economic objectives may become the central concern of similar contestations in the political arena. Indeed, this view does, albeit erratically, enter into Nolutshungu's argument, for he contends (following Poulantzas) that social classes, although essentially economic, are also always ideological and political. Furthermore, the economic system and the social division of labour, Nolutshungu insists, must be conceived of as always simultaneously economic, ideological and political:

> It is simply impossible to make sense of the ideological and political effectiveness of class divisions, or to understand the real boundaries of classes outside of the immediate site of production, unless one recognizes that politics and ideology (which are not simply reflections of the economic) also have their important effects on the total meaning of class. (p.51)

> . . . racial phenomena are not merely ideological epiphenomena but, in the colonial heritage of South Africa, an integral component of the relations of domination and *exploitation at their most fundamental level – of the social division of labour* (p.63, *my emphasis*)

But if this is so then it would seem that the autonomy of the political cannot be found simply in the distinctiveness of the concerns in that terrain and it is, therefore, necessary to turn to a second point suggested by Nolutshungu concerning the specificity of the *structure* of the political. He emphasizes the importance, in the field of political class antagonism, of the '. . . topography of the (political) field itself . . .' His object is

> . . . to define the place of politics in the general problem of change in South Africa, to indicate how the objective material inequalities between Black and White create formidable political problems for any partial resolution of the conflict that is based on elite incorporation, and to illustrate the political and ideological resistances that have been established by tradition and by *the nature of the political terrain* (p.xi, *my emphasis*).

He has, however, virtually nothing more to say about this by way of elaboration. He makes passing references to the notion of institutional structure and the form of the state, to various generalities about cultural and linguistic elements but there is *very* little analysis of the structure of the political field in terms of its institutional and organisational order and he does not analyse '. . . the institutions or mechanisms of control and regulation . . .' (p.50).

Thus, Nolutshungu's attempt to define the specificity of the political system in terms of both of its particular pre-occupations *and* its structures turns out to be inadequate because (i) he is unable to advance a convincing argument that certain issues must be regarded as the exclusive concern of the political system and (ii) he fails to demarcate the structural distinctiveness of the political system or its relevance to an account of contemporary political conflict; this would have required an analysis of the institutional and organisational structure of the state and the political terrain which Nolutshungu does not offer. I will return to these issues in Chapter 4.

If Nolutshungu does, at least, raise the issue of the structure of the political sphere, Davis and Bob Fine (1985, and see also Bob Fine 1984), by contrast, see no necessity for a structural analysis. They address this question through a critique of the notion of *structural periodisation*.

The concept of periodisation is a concept pertinent to the analysis of historical discontinuity since it signals the possibility that the historical development of a society, or sectors of it such as the economy or polity, may be demarcated by periods which differ in significant respects from one another. What is to be regarded as significant will vary, as the social science literature testifies, according to the purpose of the periodisation and on the theoretical standpoint deployed. For example, difficult as it may be to reach an agreed empirical conclusion about any particular society, from a Marxist standpoint the transition from capitalism involves a periodisation based on structural considerations – fundamental restructuring of the relations of production and the political system.

But does a structural periodisation of the South African political system since 1948, either on its own or as part of a more encompassing analysis, provide an adequate foundation upon which political strategies in the current situation may be properly formulated?

Davis and Bob Fine argue that a structural periodisation is not only insufficient; it must be rejected because it produces an account of the situation which exaggerates its rigidity and consequently leads to the neglect of the transformative force of struggles. Instead, in order to ground a critical analysis of the politics of the national liberation movement in the 1950s, they implicitly base a periodisation of post-1948 politics on the character of the political struggles of the period: the mass struggles of 1948 to 1961; small scale underground political and armed struggles in the following ten years or so.

They are content merely to describe the content of the mass struggles and analyse the strategies employed without reference to the structural conditions in which these events took place, although they do, in principle, make a gesture towards these conditions. In what follows, my purpose is to show the inadequacy of the attempt to deal with political conflicts in isolation from an analysis of the structural context – a context which both conditions and may be conditioned by these conflicts.

The starting point from which Davis and Bob Fine begin their discussion is unexceptionable. They argue that the outcome of political struggles cannot be explained by 'objective factors' alone (for example, size of the working class, strength of the state's repressive apparatus) nor by 'subjective factors' alone (for example, commitment to the struggle, brutality of the dominant classes). Furthermore, not even a combination of both is sufficient. What has to be taken into account is a factor which is part of neither the 'subjective' nor the 'objective' conditions, at least as defined by them. This is 'the conscious rational side of social movements' (p.26). They are at pains, however, to stress that:

> In explaining failure, it is as mistaken, in our view, to exclude the strategic direction taken by a movement, as it is to hold it entirely responsible, as if the 'correct strategy' would always guarantee success. (p.26)

It follows, therefore, that the question at issue relates to how the movement's strategy is to be understood in relation to the conditions which are external to it – such as, but not only, the conditions which Davis and Bob Fine have labelled 'subjective' and 'objective'. But, as I will try to show, they actually make no serious attempt either to specify properly these external conditions or to indicate how they are to be taken into account. In fact, these conditions, even in the limited terms defined by them and described above, disappear from both their brief theoretical discussion and from their empirical analysis of three important contemporary historical episodes.

The disappearance of these conditions and the absence of an account of the political structures from their analysis is no accident. As I showed in an earlier article (Wolpe 1985), Bob Fine's (1984) analysis of trade union law and the state's role in relation to the black trade unions turns entirely on the question of struggle. He argues that the effect of the law will be determined by trade union struggles; but the conditions in which these struggles occur, including the legal conditions (for example, the proscriptions written into the law, the position of the judiciary in relation to the executive, parliament and security forces and so on) are given no weight.

A similar line of argument is followed in the Davis and Bob Fine 1985 article. What is at issue, they argue, in explaining the success or failure of a social movement, is how a social movement imposes its 'own definition on the social conditions and popular consciousness which it finds as its objective presuppositions' (p.27). Furthermore, they contend, strategies are expressions of the 'movement's composition, organisation and leadership'(p.27).

These formulations lead us to pose two questions: firstly, is the movement's success or failure in imposing its own definition on the 'objective pre-suppositions' conditioned at all by these pre-suppositions and, if so, how are we to take them into account? Secondly, is it suggested that it is *only* the composition, organisation and leadership of the movement which determines strategies or do the 'objective pre-suppositions' play any role in this and, if so, how are we to understand that role?

In fact, Davis and Bob Fine restrict their attempt to theorise these questions to a critique of my work on the South African state and the periodisation of apartheid [8]. I have already indicated that there is virtually no discussion of the relevant issues in the South African political literature. For the most part, the work simply focuses on either the structures (compare, for example, Davis, 1979) or on the struggles. It is for this reason that a discussion of Davis and Bob Fine's comments is both appropriate and necessary.

They contend that the work they are criticising provides a theorisation of the political analysis of the national liberation movement. In this work, they argue, each period is presented

> ... as characterised by a definite form of state which in turn
> determines the nature of the struggle possible from below. (p.28)

Although the argument is by no means clear, it appears that their major objection is to the determining role seemingly given to the state to shape political struggles, rather than to the identification of a definite form of state. That is to say, to give this role to the state entails a failure to understand that the form of state has its origins in the class struggle. This error, they suggest, follows from the method adopted:

> The state, Wolpe suggests, is either the product or the determinant of class struggle. It cannot be both. Wolpe counterposes the question of the determination of class struggles by the state to that of the determination of the state by class struggle. (p.28)

It is clear from the above quotation that Davis and Fine wish to argue that the state is both determinant of and determined by the class struggle. They suggest that the failure to understand this leads to a failure of explanation:

> ... the same form of state which Wolpe saw as crucial in explaining the turn to armed struggle in the 1960s – in particular the subordination of the state in general to the military and bureaucracy – was not capable of preventing the revival of a mass movement in the 1980s. (p.21)

I will leave till later a more accurate and fuller account of my own position and an explanation of how mass struggles were able to re-surface. Here I want to trace through one aspect of Davis and Bob Fine's argument.

If, in fact, the argument was that the form of state is the single determinant of the political struggle, then the revival of the mass movement under the same form of state (on the assumption, which may not be tenable, that the structure of the state in fact remained unchanged) has obliterated that movement would, indeed, signal a failure of explanation. But that was not the argument. The question I was concerned with was: what is the effect of, not only the form of state, but also the structure of the political terrain on the organisational and strategic possibilities in a particular period? The answer suggested was that once the military and bureacratic apparatuses had become superordinate in the state and had obliterated the terrain of extra-parliamentary politics, then certain severe constraints were placed on the possibilities of struggle. This was not to argue that, within this form of political system, changes might not occur which would lead to transformations in the situation and hence to openings for political action.

The problem with the approach adopted by Davis and Bob Fine is that it confines them entirely to a concern with origins and not at all with the effects or outcome of struggles. It is for this reason that they are unable to take account of particular structural forms once they are established. Thus although they claim to be concerned with the effects of class struggles, their pre-occupation is with the description of struggles – the effect of previous struggles, for example, in leading to the establishment of a particular form of state never surfaces in their account. They content themselves with the argument that everything is vulnerable to the class struggle. But this merely brings us back to the question: Under what conditions do these struggles occur; what are the conditions which structure them and affect their outcome?

Of particular importance in this regard is the question of the form or structure of the political terrain in addition to the question of the form of the state (a distinction which is rarely made in the literature). Davis and Bob Fine actually only refer to the latter aspect but, implicitly, they collapse the distinction. They say:

> The difficulty in our view, is that Wolpe tends to abstract the effects of law and state from the class relations within which they are imbricated and from the social forces they seek to express and mould. (p.29)

The functional implications of this statement are clear and not only from the comment that the law and state seek to 'express' class relations. Clearly, the implicit conception of the state and law is an instrumental one in which there is no room for conflict and contradictions within and between state apparatuses and between the state and struggles on the political terrain – the state simply gives effect to the class struggles carried out in the terrain of politics.

CONCLUSION

In this chapter the discussion has focused on three major obstacles to the development of more penetrating analyses of the South African state and political terrain. These impediments are not the preserve of any one specific theoretical framework but are to be found, admittedly in various guises and with different consequences, in all the major approaches current in South African political analysis. Thus, the over-emphasis of historical continuity surfaces in some of the liberal, Marxist and black consciousness literature as well as in the popular writings of political organisations and the media. Likewise, the conception of primordial racial motivations is the foundation of race reductionism but is also found, for example, in some interpretations of the theory of internal colonialism which derive from a very different, Marxist, approach. Similarly, an economic reductionist conception of class operates across different frameworks as does the tendency to neglect the analysis of structural conditions.

In the following chapters, the effect of these obstacles will be dealt with at a more concrete level in the course of elaborating a more fruitful approach which, in many important respects, is already present, in certain parts of the literature devoted to South Africa.

# 2 Differing Conceptions of the Economy, the State and Politics in South Africa

INTRODUCTION

The previous chapter served to identify three theoretical obstacles which function with adverse effects in a great deal of South African analysis. In this chapter I want to indicate the obstructive effects of these obstacles through an examination of specific analyses of the political system which are significant because of their bearing on the political strategies of different social forces or political movements.

The discussion falls into two sections, each concerned with a different issue. In the first, the focus is on two different characterisations of the South African social formation and the alternative political perspectives which are derived from these. The section begins with a brief examination of the liberal modernisation thesis which envisages an evolutionary demolition of apartheid as the necessary outcome of the contradiction between political racial domination and the processes of the market economy. The conditions under which this gives way to reformist politics is also touched on.

This is followed by a discussion of the theory of internal colonialism or colonialism of a special type (CST). According to this theory, racial domination is not in contradiction to, but a condition of capitalist development in South Africa. This implies a rejection of the contention that class and race constitute autonomous and opposing phenomena, yet, as will be shown, the terms in which the theory is expressed allow for certain ambiguities, which permit alternative and inconsistent political perspectives to be formulated.

In the second section, the question in issue is: how are the state and political terrain portrayed? Two views of the South African state will be examined. The first, which may be labelled neo-Poulantzian, since it draws on a particular (and erroneous) interpretation of the work of N.Poulantzas [1], is concerned primarily with the relationship between the dominant classes and the form of state. The second deals with theories of South African fascism and, in particular, the analysis of the structure of the state. It will be shown that (i) the neo-Poulantzian analysis does not advance our understanding of the South African state because it actually fails to address the question of the form or structure of the state and (ii) insofar as the theory of South African fascism does deal with the structure of the state, its treatment is defective, in particular because it underestimates the effect of racially exclusive democratic structures on the functioning of the state as a whole and, furthermore, (iii) that neither approach is concerned with the character of the political terrain.


LIBERAL MODERNISATION THEORY: THE CONTRADICTION BETWEEN
CAPITALISM AND RACISM

In explicit rejection of economic reductionist theories, the liberal view, at least in its politically most important version, argues that the structure of white domination originates, on the basis of the principle of race, outside the economy within the political sphere. It has already been argued, in Chapter 1, that it is incorrect and unilluminating to see the political order as being organised exclusively or overwhelmingly around the principle of race: it leads to an over-simplified view of the racial order by omitting the social, political and economic differentiation which exists within and between racially defined groups and which have profound consequences for the latter. I now want to draw out a different aspect of this liberal analysis.

The fundamental presupposition of the liberal theory under consideration is that the racial order is essentially a political/ideological phenomenon. It originates, and is reproduced, outside the modern industrial or capitalist economy. In this view, the racial order is governed by irrational orientations. For example, social relations are based not on the qualities (including educational and other qualifications) attained by individuals in the process of their social development and which equip them to fill certain roles but, rather on attributes assumed to be possessed by individuals by virtue of birth into and membership of a racial group. Thus, by way of illustration, the right to vote is accorded on the basis of the presence or absence of ascribed, particularistic – racial – attributes rather than on the basis of universal criteria such as literacy or political knowledge.

By contrast to this irrationality of the political racial order, the industrial economy is essentially rational. It is governed by the allocation of resources, both material and human, in terms of a strict calculation of the means required to achieve particular ends, production and profit. For example, in the economy, the placement of individuals in occupations will be based on acquired qualifications and skills appropriate to the job; or, at least there will be powerful, perhaps irrepressible, pressures in that direction. Furthermore, the extent to which the qualifications and skills are possessed by any specific individual can be measured by general, universally accepted, criteria such as examinations. The particularistic attributes of race, gender, and religion are, from this rational standpoint, irrelevant and irrational.

The contention that the racial order is an irrational, political order which develops and is reproduced outside of the economy, makes it possible for liberal theory to posit a double relationship between white domination and the rational industrial or capitalist economy.

On the one hand, precisely because of its inherent irrationality, the racial order operates in contradiction to the rational, modernising tendencies of the economy.

On the other hand, although the racial order arises outside of the economy, it has nonetheless been able in South Africa to assert its contradictory effects within the economy. Having developed *sui generis*, the racial order, utilising the state as its instrument, at least during a long period, imposes itself over and within the economy. As Horwitz (1967) states:

> ... the South African economy of the 1960s has been decisively shaped, and perhaps determined, ... by an overpowering pursuit of ideas, or ideology ... The polity has always sought its ideal and ideology – the White man's supremacy. The network of economic development had to follow accordingly. (p.10–11)

The economy, that is to say, is made to 'fit' the imperatives of the racialised political system. But in securing this 'fit' through the insertion of racial criteria into the economy (for example, the operation of racial discrimination in the labour market, the exercise of monopoly control, by way of racial exclusiveness, over skilled jobs, and so forth) the political system, based on race, acts as a fetter on and distorts the economy. It inhibits the realisation of economic rationality. There is, that is to say, a contradiction between the racial political system and the rationalizing tendencies of the economy such that the efficient functioning of the economy is impaired.

However, despite the dominance of the racial political system, the rationalising imperatives of the industrial economy will finally assert themselves and, in the long run, will succeed in dissolving the racial structures and their irrational intervention into the economy. At the same time a more democratic and less stratified social order will be brought into being. In Horwitz's (ibid, p.427) words the economy urges the '... polity forward beyond its (racial) ideology'. (For a similar and complementary argument see Rostow, 1960; and O'Dowd, 1978).

Thus, in a rather curious slide from a political to an economic reductionism, the theory asserts that, ultimately, the dominance of the racial political system will be subverted by an economic movement which necessarily operates in contradiction to it. It follows that, *left to its own devices*, the capitalist economy will subordinate the racialised political system and transform it to serve the needs of the 'free market'.

In this conception, it is clear, politics has no role to play in the process of social transformation. It is the modernising imperatives of the industrial economy which brings in its wake a reform of the political order. For this reason the structures of the political sphere (other than as a racial order temporarily inhibiting economic growth) are of little interest and receive virtually no attention in the academic elaboration of this approach or in the political policies derived from it.

While the belief that 'left to itself' the economy will dissolve those features of white domination which impede capitalist economic development, implies, at least, a limited opposition to apartheid, it also provides a recipe for non-intervention in the political struggle against it. It is of significance, therefore, that this conception flourished precisely under conditions in which economically powerful sections of capital (for example, in mining and agriculture) were especially dependant, for high rates of profit, on extreme forms of racial repression which secured the conditions of reproduction of a cheap black labour force. In this period the political opposition, where it existed, of these sections of capital to apartheid was extremely muted. This, it should be noted, is not to argue that mining and agricultural capital as such constructed the liberal modernisation theory of change through economic growth [2]; it is merely to suggest, that until recently, the extant political and economic situation provided favourable conditions for the currency of such a theory or ideology.

What is noteworthy, however, is that in recent years, in the face of changed political and economic circumstances, which will be discussed more fully in Chapters 4 and 5, inside South Africa this faith in the liberalising force of the economy has tended to evaporate and to be replaced by a reformist intervention in the political arena. [3]

Briefly the reasons for this are that in contemporary South Africa, for certain white class fractions, the maintenance of capitalism has become detachable from the maintenance of white domination. Provided that is, that this can be effected without endangering the reproduction of a reformed capitalist order. In this situation, the argument that white domination is a necessary and inescapable condition of the survival of capitalism in South Africa, begins to be put in question.

Despite certain contradictory effects (e.g. racism limited the growth of the home market and hence retarded the development of manufacturing during the period of economic dominance of mining and farming capital), white domination was a fundamental condition of the reproduction of an historically particular economic and political configuration of capitalist development in which mining and farming were dominant in the economy and dependent on cheap black labour. In the latter part of that period, white political domination, which

27

achieved a 'stable' political situation by the extreme repression of extra-parliamentary politics and the near destruction of black and oppositional political organisations and trade unions, was the condition of a rapid expansion and reproduction of a particular racialised form of economy. This political economy also served, although unequally (and, indeed, with contradictory effects) different fractions of capital and other white classes. The conditions in this period, of which the above are not exhaustive, were favourable to the propagation among certain white class fractions of an ideology of political passivity in relation to the demands for the dismantling of white domination.

However, the development of capitalism itself produced conditions such that the 'positive' effects of white domination for the further development of certain capitalist interests began, increasingly, to become subordinated to negative or contradictory effects, at least in so far as the now economically dominant fractions of capital, and dependent section of other classes, for example, the white merchants, are concerned. There are two aspects to this. Firstly, the massive expansion of manufacturing, the growth in the demand for certain types of labour and the importance of the home market to the further expansion of manufacturing and merchant capital began to lead certain class fractions to perceive apartheid as an obstacle to their further expansion. Secondly, the rise of the black trade union movement and the revitalization and expansion of the mass struggles and organisations put the politics of white domination into question for these class fractions since it entails considerable costs and extreme political instability which threaten the reproduction of the entire social system.

In this way, the old view has been, as it were, falsified by historical events. The processes, political and economic, of capitalist development did not lead to the predicted evolutionary change, only to intensified conflict. The social, political and ideological conditions have now rendered obsolete the old theory and, in particular, have undermined the radical separation previously drawn between the polity and the economy. In this new period, conditions have emerged which foster interventionist ideologies and policies and, indeed, these have found their expression, in the case of corporate capital, in the reformist policies of the Progressive Reform Party, various business organisations such as the Associated Chambers of Commerce, the Urban Foundation and other organisations. This aspect will be discussed further in Chapter 5.

COLONIALISM OF A SPECIAL TYPE

It was suggested earlier, in Chapter 1, that the characterisation of South Africa as a 'colonialism of a special type' or an 'internal colonialism' reflects the confluence of two theoretical and two corresponding political currents – on the one hand, representations of the divisions in the society in terms of concepts of race which provided the basis for a politics of African nationalism; on the other hand, analyses of South African capitalism and its location in the imperialist system leading to a politics of class struggle. [4]

The notion of colonialism of a special type reflects not merely a juxtaposition of two separate theoretical traditions and two associated political objectives, national liberation and socialism, but a reformulation, which incorporates fundamental elements, of the previously discrete, not necessarily congruent, perspectives into a new theory of the South African social formation. This conception received concrete expression in a common programme, the *Freedom Charter* adopted in 1955. At the theoretical level this opened the way for the development of a new conception of the relationship between race and class.

The liberal writer Leo Marquard (1957) was the first to describe South Africa as an internal colonialism. For Marquard, the internal colonial structure was exclusively a racial, political and ideological phenomenon which has no relationship with, or bearing on, the South African economy. It is more particularly in this latter respect that the theory of colonialism of a special type developed by the national liberation movement differs from the liberal position. Colonialism of a special type defines the co-existence and articulation of a colonial relation between black and white people and a developed capitalist economy within the confines of a single national state.

Internal colonialism owes its origins to the 'decolonisation' of South Africa in 1910. The Union of South Africa came into being as an independent state as the result of the South Africa Act passed by the British Parliament in 1909. National sovereignty, however, was vested in a white state and a racially exclusive political system. The capitalist economy of South Africa was already in the hands of British capital and an indigenous white capitalist class. A system of internal colonialism was set in place which, in the course of its development, entrenched and reinforced the political subjugation of the black majority and provided the conditions for the capitalist exploitation of the black people by both foreign and white-owned national capital. Colonialism of a special type has been defined as follows:

> On one level, that of 'white South Africa', there are all the features of an advanced capitalist state in its final stage of industrial monopolies and the merging of industrial and finance capital ... But on another level, that of 'Non-White South Africa', there are all the features of a colony. The indigenous population is subjected to extreme national oppression, poverty and exploitation, lack of all democratic rights and political domination ... *Non-White South Africa is the colony of white*

29

> *South Africa itself.'* (ANC Strategy and Tactics in the South
> African Revolution in *ANC Speaks,* 1977)

The all important point, then, which demarcates the theory of
colonialism of a special type from the liberal conception is the
identification of the linkages between the colonial structure and the
capitalist economy:

> The institutions, laws and practices of apartheid are basically
> extra-economic devices elaborated to secure the processes of
> capital accumulation through the maintenance of the black
> majority as an easily exploitable source of cheap labour power.
> Because of the total inter-penetration of racial oppression and
> capitalist exploitation, the South African struggle also necessa-
> rily has a class dimension. (ANC, n.d. p.3)

The are a number of aspects of the theory of internal colonialism
which require elaboration. Firstly, the colonial structure of the social
formation is embodied in the political, ideological and generally, the
'extra-economic devices' which operate to subordinate the black
population as a whole to the white population as a whole. The
organising principle of this structure is the definition of racial subjects
endowed with unequal rights, obligations, powers and so forth. The
society is divided into a superordinate category of white subjects and a
subordinate category of black subjects. The parallel with 'normal'
colonialism is clear: just as the colonial power, as such, can be seen to
be the oppressor of the entire colonial people, so the white state/
people are the oppressors of the entire black people.

It does not follow that these racial categories are internally
undifferentiated. On the contrary, there are class divisions within each
category and these give rise to different interests and political conflicts
within the racial groups. Indeed, because the black working class is
subject to the most intense exploitation, it is defined as the leading
and major agent of struggle. Nonetheless, the over-riding factor is the
racial division. It is this which ensures the advance of the interests of
all white classes against those of all black classes. This is reflected in
two ways. First, the effect of internal colonialism has been to produce
an asymetrical class structure. Class formation within the white
group is, more or less, comparable to that of other advanced capitalist
societies – an economically powerful capitalist class with both
monopoly and competitive capitalist fractions, a large class of small
producers and businessmen, a large middle stratum of clerical,
administrative, white collar and tertiary sector employees as well as a
skilled manual work force. Among the black people, there is virtually
no capitalist class, few skilled workers, and a small and relatively
under-developed petite-bourgeoisie.

Over and above this, at each point in the class structure, the situation of black classes, where they have emerged, is vastly inferior to that of corresponding white classes whatever criteria of measurement is adopted – amount of capital, wages and income, skills, productive property, and so on. Although he was writing about the black middle strata Slovo's formulation (1976) is generalisable to all black classes:

> In the case of the black middle strata, however, class mobility cannot proceed beyond a certain point; and, again, this point is defined in race rather than in economic terms. (p.126)

The colonial structure thus guarantees the superior position and dominance of the white bloc as a whole and with it the specific interests of the different classes within that bloc. Correspondingly, it reproduces the subordinate position of the black group and the different classes within it. Each class is, thus, riven by racial divisions and the fate of different classes, within each racial group, is tied to the maintenance or destruction of racial domination. Again to quote Slovo (1976):

> Objectively speaking . . . the objective fate of the black middle sections is linked much more with that of black workers and peasants than with their equivalent across the colour line. (p.126)

This has profound political consequences for it grounds the contention that the anti-racial or national struggle must have primacy in the South African context.

The primacy of the national struggle, however, must be understood in relation to the second major element of the theory of colonialism of a special type, namely, its insistence upon the functionality of the colonial structure for the expanded reproduction of capitalism in South Africa. It was indicated earlier in this section that the theory of internal colonialism argues that racial domination secures the conditions of capital accummulation not merely through an 'external' relation but also through its 'inter-penetration' of capitalist exploitation.

This has been interpreted to mean that in South Africa, capitalism cannot exist except in a racialised form protected by white domination. In one version, this argument takes, so to speak, a theoretical or conceptual form: in South Africa, it argues, capitalist relations are, by definition, *inescapably* capitalist and racial. It follows that the anti-racial, or national struggle is necessarily also a struggle against the capitalist order. In passing, it is to be noted that the absorption of race into capitalist relations in this way leads to the assumption of historical continuity, criticised in Chapter 1, because it functions to close off questions about the possible separation of and contradictions between capitalism and race.

The second version does not begin with a concept of racial capitalism, but nevertheless argues that the correlation of forces is such as to render it politically impossible for racial domination to become detached from capitalist relations. That is to say, while in principle capitalism and racialism are separable, the interpenetration which has occurred in practice and, most importantly, the vested interest of powerful groups and class forces in racial domination, are such as to make the de-racialisation of capitalism unrealisable. As Slovo (1976) has expressed it:

> It is precisely because in South Africa capitalist production relations are the foundation of national repression that the national struggle itself has an objective coincidence with the elimination of all forms of exploitation. (p.140)

It will be argued in Chapter 3 that the proposition that there is a contingent, not a necessary, relationship between capitalism and racism in South Africa is a correct starting point. However, the identification of the national struggle with the struggle against capitalism, whether rooted in the concept of racial capitalism or in an empirical judgment about their inseparability, has the effect of closing off the analysis of the class content of national struggles – even in the conditions of South Africa the national struggle does not necessarily have a single, anti-capitalist connotation; it will be given a different content by different classes.

The immediately preceding argument has suggested that by linking capitalism and racial domination in an inescapable relationship, the internal colonial thesis may lead to the conclusion that the socialist revolution is a necessary ingredient of the national liberation struggle. This results in a failure to recognise that the national struggle and, indeed, anti-racist movements may incorporate alternative class objectives.

A similar failure follows from the over-emphasis sometimes given to the contention, within the internal colonialism thesis, that racial domination serves to bind the classes within each racial group to a common struggle to maintain or overthrow that domination. As I have noted, the theory of colonialism of a special type recognises the common interest of classes within racial groups in maintaining or eliminating racial boundaries and that simultaneously class interests are differentially served or blocked by these boundaries. In some formulations of the political objectives which flow from the internal colonial thesis, the latter aspect tends to be forgotten. The consequence is to present the struggle for national liberation as if it were free of class implications. In fact, in this event, a radical separation between the national and the class struggle is re-introduced and, once again, the question of the class content of the national struggle is submerged. The presumption is that the class question, the question of capitalism or socialism, will be settled after the national democratic state has been established and that it is not directly implicated in the national struggle itself.

This view is, of course, a particular representation of the notion of a two-stage revolution which is the subject of debate between different currents in the contemporary struggle against apartheid.

The opposite error is committed by some writers who fall within those tendencies which may be labelled as 'ultra left' or 'workerist'. For them, the national struggle cannot be an ingredient of the workers' struggle. National liberation and socialism stand in contradiction to one another. The implied reason for this is that nationalism is assumed to 'belong' to the bourgeoisie or the petite-bourgeoisie in its endeavours to become a bourgeoisie; nationalism can have only one, bourgeois, class content, and can serve the class interests of only one class.

The reductionism and economism of this view are patent. On the one hand, nationalism is reduced to an instrument of the economic/political interests of only one class, the bourgeoisie; on the other hand, the working class is portrayed as having 'purely' economic interests deriving from the shop floor. The supposition that, for the working class, the class struggle and the national liberation struggle stand in contradiction to one another has significant implications for it leads to the supposition that the 'correct' political perspective is a 'pure' class struggle with the working class alone going for socialism.

Is it adequate simply to set the class struggle *against* the national struggle? The question we have to pose is: what is the class content of the national struggle or, more accurately, what are the class interests bound up with specific formulations of the national question? It is quite clear that the national struggle may have a conservative or reformist or bourgeois content. But, it follows from what has been said, that there are no theoretical grounds for denying the possibility of revolutionary nationalism which has as its objective both national liberation and socialism.

Be that as it may, what is absolutely clear in the contemporary period is that no section of the national liberation movement is committed to or struggles for, what may be termed, a bourgeois national democratic revolution. Even the conception of the two-stage revolution referred to above, the main target of the 'left'/'workerist' contention that the national liberation movement is bourgeois in character, has nothing in common with the vision of corporate capital or, say, the bantustan sections of the black petite-bourgeoisie for a de-racialised capitalist South Africa. The two-stage revolution does not envisage a transformation based merely on a degree of redistribution of wealth and political power in favour of the black people; it envisages the first stage as merely a stage in which the conditions are established which will permit the inauguration of a process of further social transformation. Jordan (1983) has expressed the point as follows:

> . . . the Freedom Charter, though not itself a socialist document or programme, lays the basis for the seizure and holding of political power by the oppressed in South Africa. The radical measures of agrarian reform, and nationalisation it entails will go a long way towards removing the commanding heights of the economy from the sphere of private ownership and open up the way for the socialist transformation of our country. However, the pre-condition for all this is the revolutionary overthrow of the Pretoria racist regime. (p.11)

This quite different understanding of the theory of internal colonialism and the conception of stages of revolution is clearly shown in the documents of the liberation movement and in alternative interpretations. Although, the ANC for example does not purport to be engaged in a struggle for socialism, its interpretation of the Freedom Charter, as Jordan has contended, is not empty of class implications. That is to say, the national liberation struggle is seen to have a certain class content:

> . . . the ANC has always considered the two economic clauses of the Freedom Charter: 'The People Shall Share in the Country's Wealth' and 'The Land Shall Be Shared Amongst Those Who Work It' to be the very core of its revolutionary programme. These clauses envisage the seizure of economic assets, presently owned and controlled either by individual capitalists or capitalist companies drawn from the white minority or transnational corporations. (ANC, n.d. p.3)

The Communist Party (1986) formulates its position more sharply:

> The working class, who take the lead in the struggle are equally concerned to establish a socialist transformation which . . . will free all of society from exploitative social relations.
>
> In order to create the conditions for such transformation, it is vital that we strengthen the united front of national liberation led by the ANC to overthrow white supremacy and establish an independent state of national democracy. It is not just any state that is envisaged by the Freedom Charter with its programme of profound agrarian transformation and the socialisation of those sectors of the economy in the grip of monopoly capital. This

destruction of the colonial state is the basis for working class advance. (p.12)

However, it does not follow from the fact that the liberation movement endows the national struggle with a particular class significance that other social agents, in pursuing a policy aimed to dismantle apartheid will pursue a similar objective. The development of political alliances between an aspiring black bourgeoisie and corporate capital in the changed conditions of the contemporary period in South Africa underscores the importance of opening up the question of the specific class content of variant formulations of policies aimed at dismantling the structure of racial domination. As indicated above, this will be further discussed in the next chapter.

THE FORM OF THE CAPITALIST STATE IN SOUTH AFRICA

*Introduction*
In the previous section, the discussion centred largely on two approaches which are based on fundamentally different views of the relationship between the capitalist economy and the racial order. These differences lead to vastly divergent political perspectives or objectives. Liberal modernisation theory gives rise to a concern with the reform of the political system which, either through the imperatives of the economy or through political intervention, will liberate the economy from the irrationality of race and open the way for the development of a de-racialised, and hence more egalitarian, rational free market system.

The theory of colonialism of a special type, on the other hand, generates a concern with the revolutionary overthrow of white domination to be accompanied by, or as a precursor to, a radical, if not socialist, transformation of the capitalist order.

In both cases, therefore, the focus was on the concerns or objectives which come to be defined in the political terrain. Or, to put it somewhat differently, the political terrain appears to be defined solely in terms of political concerns or the object of struggles.

It was argued in part 3 of Chapter 1, however, that it is not sufficient to concentrate only on the character of political struggles to the exclusion of the political structures. The question, then, that has to be addressed to both approaches relates to their account of the political structures.

In general, at the political level, to the extent that concepts of structure are deployed, both theories are pre-occupied with the racialisation of the structures – the exclusion of blacks from the franchise, the reservation of senior ranks in the army and police to white people, the segregation of educational institutions and so forth.

This, undoubtedly, is of fundamental importance but it by no means exhausts what needs to be identified in terms of the structures of the political system.

Thus, the form of the state – the relations between legislature, executive and judiciary, and of the military to all of these – the organisational and institutional structure of the terrain of politics external to the state structures and so on, are not reducible merely to their racial content. Nevertheless, the analysis of other structural conditions tends to be relatively neglected in the political writings or to be treated in a rather ad hoc manner. To develop a more adequate analysis of the political sphere, the state and the political terrain, it is necessary to turn largely to a different literature.

Firstly, the debate among academic writers on the theoretical analysis of the South African state. Two currents dominated that debate. The first, based on the so-called capital logic approach simply posited the state as the instrument of 'capital-in-general' and, as a consequence, had virtually nothing to say about the form or structure of the state.[5] Of considerably greater interest is the second current which claimed to take as its starting point Poulantzas's version of the relationship between the power bloc and the form of the capitalist state. This work is seriously flawed in a number of respects; nevertheless it represents one of the few attempts to develop a theoretical analysis of the South African state and an examination of it makes it possible to advance the debate in a different, and more fruitful, direction.

Secondly, a body of literature on the theme of South African fascism. While the term is widely used in the political statements of the national liberation movement, it has been elaborated in the academic work of Simson (1980) and in a much more directly political intervention by Bunting (1964). This work, too, has certain shortcomings the analysis of which will, again, serve to contribute to the task of developing a more adequate approach.

*The Power Bloc and the Form of the State*
In a book (Davis 1979) and a number of articles (see Davies et al, 1976; Kaplan, 1976) purporting to be based on the work of Poulantzas, the form, that is the structure, of the state is denoted by the class composition of the power bloc and the specific class or class fraction which is hegemonic within that bloc. The structure of the state is to be found in the specific contradictory and asymmetrical relations between the classes which constitute the power bloc. Empirically, the analysis of the changing form or structure of the state is focused, quite logically given the starting point, particularly on the periodic changes of the hegemonic class or class fraction and this, in turn, is demonstrated by shifts in state policies. Since the policies which come to be adopted by

the state express the interests of specific classes or class fractions, they indicate which of these has become hegemonic. Hence, changing policies signal changes in the power bloc and this reflects changes in the structure of the state. Davis et al. attempt to demonstrate this through an account of the struggles between mining capital and national capital over free trade and protectionist policies – a protectionist policy indicated that national capital had become hegemonic, while free trade policies indicated a shift to mining capital. In both cases a change in state form is held to have occurred.

In this account, the state is represented as a simple, unified instrument which operates, unequivocally, to meet the needs of the hegemonic class fraction.

In the words of Davis et al (1976, p.5):

> ... the state and state power cannot be divided and parcelled out among the classes/fractions within the power bloc. *State power is a unity, requiring organisational direction to be effective.* Thus, there is always a struggle within the power bloc to assume this organisational role, and thereby ensure the primacy of this class/fraction's particular interests. (*emphasis added*)

The reduction of the structure of the state to the relation between the dominant classes and their struggles over policy, has the result that the apparatuses which constitute the state are never put in issue. Instead, it is simply assumed that there is a unity of function and a single purpose (to give effect to the interests of the hegemonic class). But this excludes, as I will show in more detail below, an entire field of investigation – the contradictory and asymetrical relations within the matrix of state organisations and institutions and the way in which these condition and are conditioned by struggles in the political terrain.

It is precisely this position which Poulantzas tried to avoid. Poulantzas's theorisation of the capitalist state has been subjected to wide ranging criticisms, not least on the grounds that he fails to relate the state and politics properly in their relationship to the processes of capital accumulation. It is not my intention to traverse the corpus of Poulantzas's work here; rather I want to differentiate his approach from that of Davis et al. in order to emphasise how his work poses the question of the structure of the state which they, in their interpretation of Poulantzas, submerge.

Despite then, the limitations of Poulantzas's work and, in the present context, above all, the slide between a 'structuralist' and an instrumentalist conception of the state [which, however, he began to correct in his later work; see, *NLR*, 95 and *State Power and Socialism* (1979)] his concept of the state as structure does not permit a simple reduction of the form of the state to the relation of classes in the power bloc. This is made clear in the following passage:

> Institutions, considered from the point of view of power, can be related only to *social classes which hold power.* As it is exercised this power of the social classes is organised in specific institutions which are *power centres*: in this context the state is the *centre of the exercise of political power.* But this does not mean that power centres, the various institutions of an economic, political, military, cultural, etc. character are mere instruments, organs or appendices of the power of social classes. They possess their autonomy and structural *specificity* which is not as such reducible to an analysis in terms of power (Poulantzas, 1973, p.115).

The irreducibility of the structural specificity of the state to an analysis of class power (the very reduction which Davis et al make) derives from the relative autonomy of the state from the dominant classes in capitalist social formations. This, for Poulantzas, is a fundamental property of the capitalist state.

In one line of his analysis, Poulantzas bases this autonomy on the distinction between structure and class practices. It will be recalled that, for Poulantzas, classes can be conceptualized only in struggle, that is as practices. Those practices, however, are determined by an articulation of economic, political and ideological structures (the structural determination of classes), which do not themselves entail practices.

How is the structural determination of classes conceptualized in relation to the political structure of the state?

To begin with, it must be noted that Poulantzas distinguishes the state as structure from classes and class practices:

> ... the juridico-political state superstructure ... is not the same as the political class struggle ... since the state apparatuses are no more classes than are relations of production (Poulantzas, 1973, p.18).

Now, the form of the relationship between the state as political structure and social class is identical to that of the relationship between the economic and the ideological structures and classes, although the content of that relationship differs. The general form of the relationship between structure and class is expressed by Poulantzas in the following way:

> ... the concept of power specifies the effects of the ensemble of these (i.e. structural) levels on the relations between social *classes* in struggle. *It points to the effects of the structure on the*

*relations of conflict between the practices of the various classes in 'struggle'.* In other words, power is not located in the level of the structures, but is an effect of the ensemble of these levels . . . (Poulantzas, 1973, p.19).

It follows that for Poulantzas the specific form of the state is a question which has to be determined at the level of the political structures. By contrast, questions concerning the composition of the power bloc, the relations of hegemony and the struggles within it, have to be considered at the level of class practices. These latter phenomena are, in Poulantzas's argument, conditioned by the structures. Thus, the form of the state and the power bloc are seen as clearly separate yet articulated 'spheres'. In no sense is it possible, in his analysis, to reduce the form of the state to the composition of or to the relations of hegemony within the power bloc. The effects of the political structure on the class struggle are related to the specific form of the state, in particular, to the concrete distinction and relationship between the executive and legislature, but also to the institutional and organisational character of the various state ideological and repressive apparatuses and the relationship between them.

By contrast the neo-Poulantzians are pre-occupied merely with the outcome of struggles between the dominant classes, which result in the state giving effect to particular policies favoured by the hegemonic class. How the specific form of the state (for example, the relationship between judiciary, legislature and executive, the dominance over, or subordination of these to the repressive state apparatuses) conditions the struggles and what the consequences are of those struggles for the structure of the state, are not questions addressed in this approach. And this is so a *fortiori* in respect of the dominated classes since, for Davis et al., the contradiction between capital and labour takes place outside of the state, 'at a distance'. The outcome of this is an exclusive concern with conjunctural struggles always premised on the ultimate reduction of the state to a unified instrument of the hegemonic class and, therefore, a neglect of the structural form of the state. Nor does the approach make place for a specification of the political terrain outside of the state.

This paradoxical neglect of the state structures and the political terrain in work concerned with the state, is accompanied, no doubt due to the inherent economism of the approach, by an exclusive pre-occupation with the intervention of the state in the economy. The focus is entirely on questions of taxation, balance of payments, free trade versus protectionism, allocation of individuals in the occupational structure, cheap labour and so on. Important as these questions are it is nonetheless astonishing that there should be no interest in specifically political questions – for example, the national struggle, the mode of organisation of the Afrikaner Volk (but see O'Meara, 1983).

## The Concept of South African Fascism

The question of the form of the state is directly posed in the literature which characterises South Africa as a fascist society since it puts in issue not only the racist character of the political system, but also the structural form of the state and the relationship between different components of that structure. To this extent it promises to go beyond the conceptions of the political which have thus far been considered. In this section I want explore the extent to which the theory of South African fascism specifies a distinctive form or structure of the political sphere.

In general, the literature on fascism concentrates on the *origins* of the fascist order in the crisis conditions which prevailed in different countries but there has been very little interest in theorising the form of the fascist state. How far do accounts of South African fascism go to meet this shortcoming?

This is by no means a question of merely academic interest. The term 'South African Fascism' is widely used in popular descriptions of South Africa. It is also frequently employed in the literature of the national liberation movement, apparently without theoretical pretensions, as a shorthand description of the comprehensive discriminatory and repressive character of the society. Here it functions as a symbol around which opposition to the apartheid state can be mobilised. Nevertheless, the characterisation of South Africa as fascist may have other, more profound, implications for oppositional political policies and strategies. Insofar as the description of the society as fascist connotes a closing down of the space available for the organisation of struggle on the political terrain, to that extent it may lead, for example, to a strategy which emphasises the armed rather than other forms of illegal struggle. This was precisely the issue which the national liberation movement confronted in 1961 in the aftermath of Sharpeville. Again, the ANC (1987) has used the notion of South African fascism as the basis for a call to whites to join it in the struggle to dislodge the present regime.

The South Africa Communist Party analyses post-1948 South African history in terms of stages of fascism. According to this account the National Party inaugurated the process which culminated in the establishment of a fascist or police state on 'the Hitlerite model' (*African Communist* No.46, p.23). In this statement, the developed stage of fascism – the abandonment of legality and the increase in state terror – owes its origins to the defeat of the regime in 1956 with the collapse of the Treason Trial:

> The reaction of the fascist government was to discard legal procedures in favour of lawless police terrorism. The ANC was declared illegal ... The militant mass struggles of the fifties,

40

although they stopped short of violence on the part of the people, shook the ruling classes and the colonialist Apartheid structure of South Africa. Unable to continue their rule in the old way, they abandoned all pretence at bourgeois legality and took the road of naked terrorism. (p.24)

Thus, a new, more extreme phase of fascism is explained as a defensive reaction by the state to the mass struggles of the 1950s, particularly insofar as the success of the struggles was signalled by the state's defeat in the Treason Trial. However, even if we accept this as part of the explanation, is it sufficient? After all the strengthening of the military bureaucratic structure of the state and the attenuation of legality went much further after the decisive defeat of the mass movement following Sharpeville in 1960. Since increased repression followed first the upsurge of the mass movement and second its defeat, an adequate explanation must surely go beyond upsurge/defeat to a more complex analysis of the political conjuncture.

Be that as it may, the aspect I want to focus on is the contention that the essential process which produced the fascist state was the abandonment of 'bourgeois legality'. While clearly, there was a far-reaching erosion of legal rights and an expansion of administrative regulation in the post-Treason Trial period, it is also, nonetheless, true that that erosion was uneven and incomplete. The reality was more complex and that complexity can only be grasped by an analysis of the specific and differentiated changes in the law and in the structures of the state and political terrain.

Thus, for example, the decline of legality implied an alteration in the nature of different state apparatuses – for example, an expansion of the security forces and their 'modernisation', changes in the composition of the judiciary and its jurisdiction – and in the relations of dominance, autonomy, cooperation and contradiction between them. But it did not involve a total abandonment of legality in the political sphere, particularly vis à vis white politics. Furthermore, these changes were related to shifts in the relation of Parliament to the judiciary and of both to the executive with evident increases in the dominance of the latter.

This process was neither simple nor straightforward, for the inroads into the role of the judiciary were not brought about directly by the executive, but by the intervention of Parliament. Since the paramountcy of the executive was the product of legislation, one might say that the road to executive autonomy was via the assertion and enforcement of the supremacy of Parliament. Similarly, other state apparatuses (for example, bantustans, Bantu Education, labour bureaux, etc) underwent important legal changes. In short, what the statement describes as the abandonment of bourgeois legality and the introduction of a lawless mode of enforcement of repression, is only partially true and is, furthermore, to be seen as only part of a process which involved significant restructuring of the state apparatuses and of the relations between.

The legal/lawless distinction is thus too undifferentiated and too blunt a notion and does not provide adequate theoretical means for analysing the character of the state and, in particular, the fascist state.

In his book *The Rise of the South African Reich* (1964) Bunting attempts to provide an account of South African fascism through a comparison of the political-legal structure in South Africa with that which developed under Hitler in Germany. Although his book discusses a number of interesting features, it is limited in two important respects. Firstly, the method of a point by point comparison of laws amd modes of repression has the disadvantage that it tends to emphasise discrete features and to under-emphasise the structural configuration as a whole.

Secondly, since no adequate concept of fascism is specified, the features compared turn out to be ad hoc rather than theoretically selected and this undermines the possible value of the comparison.

Bunting's description of South Africa is structured, as the title of the book implies, by a particular model of fascism, namely Nazi Germany. Bunting does not elaborate that model, and his conception of fascism emerges through a series of specific analogies between the Third Reich and South Africa. This leads him to a characterisation of South African fascism in the following terms.

Firstly, the ruling National Party has brought about a situation, through a series of laws passed by Parliament, in which its continuing control of Parliament and the state bureaucracy is guaranteed. This control, interestingly enough, was not achieved by the destruction of Parliament; on the contrary, as Bunting (p.170) argues, the regime has always been 'careful to emphasise their respect for [white] Parliamentary democracy' while, at the same time, strengthening the apparatuses of coercion.

Secondly, state power has been utilised to introduce repressive measures to eliminate all extra-parliamentary opposition, to restrict freedom of speech and to control the press and publications.

In this account, then, the growth of fascism is equated with the increasing utilisation by the ruling National Party of the state as its instrument of control. It uses this instrument to extend the army and police force and to intensify repression particularly by attempting to eliminate the extra-parliamentary opposition, although it should be stressed, this occurs side by side with the retention of (white) parliamentary democracy. However, it is to be noted that the Nazification process, according to Bunting, was incomplete (in 1964, when the book was written) and he makes the curious suggestion that its perfection will depend, not on a change in the form of state and political terrain but on the development of private agencies:

South Africa is not yet Nazi Germany, with its concentration camps and gas ovens. But the attitude of mind which produced such inhumanities in Nazi Germany is there, and it needs only a whiff of a crisis for White South Africa to throw out its remaining civilized pretensions and grasp in a frenzy of panic at any weapon for preserving its privileges. If there are not yet street gangs and private armies, it is because the police have so far proved a very adequate first line of defence. (p.317) [6]

What, however, Bunting does not analyse adequately is the form of state and, as was suggested above, this is related to the fact that he does not offer a concept of fascism with which to make the analysis.

The fascist state may be said to exist in a capitalist social order (a) when the apparatuses of power (including state legislature and executive, judiciary, coercive organs and party) become fused and concentrated in such a way that they have little autonomy from one another and act as an instrument of reproduction of the system of political domination and the capitalist economy without entirely excluding the existence of continuous and, more or less, sharp contradictions and intense conflicts between the components of this 'instrument' (b) when independent organisations in the sphere of 'civil society' are eliminated or subjected to overwhelming controls such that they are unable to act as centres of opposition.

In slightly more detail, the structure of the fascist state will be constituted, inter alia, by: the extreme subordination, indeed absorption, of the legislature and judiciary to the executive; mass mobilisation by means of a fascist ideology and the representation of the masses through the party which fuses into the state apparatuses; the overwhelming development and autonomy from judicial and legislative control of the apparatuses of coercion and together with this the use of terror as a mode of operation; a corporatist form of state organisation; the virtual destruction of centres of political organisation outside of the state and party.

Clearly, a comparative analysis properly grounded may be useful as a means of posing questions about the character of the South African state. The point has already been made that the question of fascism in South Africa is not reducible to simple dichotomies (such as legal/lawless), it relates to complex structural political conditions. The object is not to fit a label, but to analyse the conditions which may be important in determining political strategies. Bunting takes some tentative steps in this direction but, in the light of the definition set out above of the structural conditions which, if applicable, would have far-reaching consequences for political practice, the restriction of his account to the dominance of the party and the elimination of extra-parliamentary organisations plus repression is manifestly unsatisfactory. [7] This is so because the focus is too narrow and, therefore, precludes a comprehensive analysis of the existence or absence of specific forms of organisational space within the political structures.

This is exemplified in his rather perfunctory discussion of one of the most difficult questions for the view that the South African state is to be identified as fascist – namely, the effects of the existence of white parliamentary democracy and of a judiciary which has never been completely subordinated to the executive. The importance of this relates to the fact that, notwithstanding the racial exclusiveness of these structures, and despite the inroads into the functioning of both, their maintenance as institutions of white politics, (perhaps particularly the judiciary) seems to have have certain limiting effects on the capacities of the executive in relation to the excluded black population. That is to say, if this is correct, apartheid is unable to impose a total *cordon sanitaire* around the effects of these institutions. Bunting refers to this but does not treat it as a problem – indeed, in the passage quoted above dealing with the full development of fascism in South Africa he does not include the elimination of the white parliamentary opposition or, for that matter, the abolition of Parliament or the total subordination of the judiciary.

Other writers have also addressed this question. Adam (1971 and 1979) has no difficulty with this because he rejects the notion of South African fascism although the grounds upon which he does so are extremely vague. He employs the notion of 'democratic police state' (or herrenvolk democracy or racial oligarchy as he variously terms it) but he merely registers these terms and does not analyse the apparently contradictory character of the structures of the state. Kaplan (1980), similarly, recognises the racially exclusive character of bourgeois democracy but is not concerned to deal with this as a problem in an analysis of the political system. He simply records the fact, but draws no conclusions. He says:

> The fact that universal suffrage does not exist in South Africa should not blind us to one important feature of the state apparatus, i.e. representation of class interests has taken place within the frame work of parliamentary democracy, While black people in South Africa have been excluded from representation within the state apparatus, Whites have enjoyed democratic representation. In short, the South African polity has been characterized by a bourgeois form of democracy, albeit of a racially exclusive kind (p.85).

It is left to Simson (1980) to try to deal with the issue but, as I will show, he simply conjures it away.

For the most part Simson has been preoccupied with the sources and content of Afrikaner 'fascist' ideology; nevertheless, in his book he sets out (a) to explain Afrikaner fascism by '. . . uncovering the social conditions of its origins' (the genetic dimension), by 'determining its objective social functions within capitalist society' (the functional dimension), and by 'explaining the ideological and organisation form of the fascist movement' (the phenomenological dimension) (p.1); and (b) to 'examine Afrikaner fascism in relation to a general theory of fascism' and to demonstrate that Christian-Nationalism is the Afrikaner variety of National Socialism in Germany and Fascism in Italy.

He introduces this discussion with the general proposition that the understanding of fascism 'necessitates a theory of crisis and transition, a theory of the state, economics, politics and ideology. Only a theoretical combination of *all* the above elements will make it possible to grasp the meaning of fascism' (p.14). Despite the ambiguity of this formulation, Simson's intention is clear – fascism is not to be understood as a simple, one-dimensional phenomenon, but as a determinate social order in which all the levels of the social formation are involved. He proceeds by providing a definition of fascism which he argues must incorporate *both* the conditions in which it comes to power and the characteristics of the fascist state and regime.

In brief, the conditions in which fascism comes to power are, generally, '. . . the rise of imperialism and monopoly capital, and the democratisation of "the masses" in a parliamentary system and trade unions' (p.14) and, specifically, a political crisis with the following characteristics: (i) 'A non-revolutionary conjuncture, i.e. the working-class is divided and on the defensive, the ruling-class is on the offensive' (p15); (ii) An hegemonic crisis of the ruling class entailing its loss of hegemony over the petite-bourgeoisie and working class masses and a consequent general ideological crisis; (iii) A crisis within the power bloc due to its inability to overcome severe internal contradictions and its inability to resolve its conflict with the masses; (iv) 'The mobilization by the fascist party of a powerful *mass movement* based predominantly on the petit-bourgeois, using a combination of legal and violent tactics and a "radical" hyper-nationalist anti-working class ideological appeal' (p.15). These crises are resolved by the establishment of a fascist order. What are the characteristics of that order?

Following Poulantzas, Simson asserts that fascism is an exceptional form of the capitalist state but, unlike Poulantzas, he makes virtually no attempt to discuss the nature of this exceptional form and we are left merely with the statement that the fascist state '. . . is distinguishable from other state forms such as bourgeois democracy, military dictatorship and Bonapartism' (p.17), without, however, a discussion of *how* they are distinguishable. Instead, Simson moves directly to a discusion of fascism as (quoting Poulantzas) ' a specific form of *regime* within the exceptional capitalist form' (p.17).

The fascist regime is generally characterised by its extreme relative autonomy from monopoly capital by virtue of the fact that it is petty bourgeois based. More specifically, the features of the fascist regime are: (a) 'A single mass party with a totalitarian guiding ideology'; (b) a subordinated trade union movement dependent on the state; (c) state apparatuses manned by members of the fascist party and 'hence the "extreme" autonomy of the state from the traditional ruling class' which enables the fascist regime to mediate the crisis 'of the power bloc and [to] establish the conditions of the hegemony of monopoly capital'; (d) increased state intervention in the economy and (e) an expanded repressive state apparatus (p.15).

Whatever the merits of this list of features, Simson undoubtedly offers more than the other protagonists of the conception of South African fascism though it is not sufficient merely to remain with this inventory. What is needed is an analysis of their combination into a system. Nowhere is this clearer than in Simson's treatment of the existence of a racially exclusive Parliament which raises awkward problems for him.

Like Bunting, Simson couples repression with restricted parliamentary democracy to characterise the South African state:

> The ... objective social function of Apartheid has been to ruthlessly suppress the rights of the African labour force (and its political leadership) and to bring it under state control. (p.198)

> Surely, the signficance of fascist 'dictatorship' is that it robs the masses of any effective voice in government and production. In South Africa, where 80% of the population lives without political representation under the heel of a regime which controls where each individual may live and work, we are certainly faced by a fascist dictatorship.

> The democracy of the Whites certainly is a 'special feature' in Afrikaner fascism and its particular effect on the functioning of society requires closer analysis. However, this feature alone is insufficient to differentiate it from classical fascism. (p.200)

Simson then attempts to provide this 'closer analysis' by simply denying its 'reality'. Thus, he argues that the fact that the big bourgeoisie and parliamentary parties retain their autonomy from the Nationalist Party in South Africa is not proof that South Africa is not a fascist society, and he disposes of the white Parliament by treating it as a functional alternative for the fascist leadership principle in which in a 'community of affinity', the leader interprets the Volks' will.

Simson is forced into this purely formal denial of significance to centres of power independent of the state (formal in the sense that their nature and significance are not analysed) and to this functional assimilation of Parliament to 'leader' (an assimilation made simply by substituting terms) because they contradict his att _npt to identify the structural feaures of South African fascism and thus cannot be accommodated within his analysis. At this point he is forced back to his main pre-occupation – fascist ideology. This he conceives of as a more or less coherent body of ideas held by the ruler, which determines the fascist character of the state. The extent to which this ideology is actually materialised in the institutional order is apparently irrelevant. Indeed, given the fascist ideology of the ruling party, nothing can displace the characterisation of the state as fascist. Hence, Parliament and independent centres of power in the political terrain are simply brushed aside.

CONCLUSION

In the first section of this chapter, attention was focused on the relationship between two theoretical accounts of the relationship between the racial political order and the economy – liberal modernisation theory and the theory of colonialism of a special type – and the varying political perspectives or objectives related to these. It was suggested that, while important theoretical and political differences emerged, the literature examined shared a common pre-occupation with political objectives, to the neglect of the structural conditions of the state and political terrain.

In the second section, two approaches to the question of the specificity of the structure of the South African state were examined. The first was based on the work of Poulantzas and the second was concerned with identifying the fascist structure of the South African state. It was shown that in the former case the analysis was unable to provide insights into the structure of the state because it tried to define the structures merely in terms of relations between the dominant classes. While the latter work did deal with state structures, it was shown that it was theoretically inadequate and, as a consequence, was unable to provide an account of the structure of the state or, for that matter, of the political terrain.

# 3 Class, Race and Political Struggle

An important objective of the review of different theoretical and political approaches in the previous chapters was to identify the limiting effects, on the substantive analysis of the South African political system, of certain theoretical formulations. Perhaps the most important point to emerge relates to what may be termed the analytical closures which are imposed, in variant ways, by the theories discussed.

Three closures were identified. Firstly, it was argued that where the political terrain is defined exclusively in terms of the conflicts which occur within it, then the analysis of the political sphere tends to be restricted to a description of the actors (classes, racial groups) who engage in, and the objectives of the struggle (reform of the capitalist order, national democratic or socialist revolution).

Secondly, it was argued that where the social order is presented as a structure of race relations which is explained in terms of concepts of race (usually conceived of as primordial), the reductionism involved ensures the systematic neglect of the role of other determinations such as class and the economy in the production of the racial order. Conversely, economic reductionist conceptions of class preclude the analysis of the phenomena of race except as a product of the economy; in this case little room is allowed for the analysis of the non-economic conditions pertinent to the formation of the social order.

Thirdly, it was argued, in relation to those approaches that conceptualise the social order in South Africa in terms of the inter-penetration of class and race, notably the theory of colonialism of a special type, that while crucial advances are made, nonetheless two closures continue to be imposed on the analysis. The supposition that capitalism in South Africa, in its *very constitution* requires the racial order which is forever necessary for its development and reproduction, precludes the search for and analysis of the uneven, asymmetrical, contradictory and unstable relations between capitalism and race. In this respect, it is of interest to note, the analysis remains on the same theoretical terrain as the liberal modernisation theory which asserts the opposite – capitalism, in its *very constitution*, is antithetical to the irrationalities of racism which inhibits its full development.

Furthermore, the contention that capitalism and the racial order are inescapably locked together is combined with the view that opposition to racial domination, the national struggle, is inevitably also locked together with opposition to capitalism. The ultra-left, so-called 'workerist' tendency, draws the opposite conclusion – for them, nationalism 'belongs' to the aspirant black bourgeoisie. Either way, what becomes obscured is the possibility that nationalist policies may differ in their class objectives. That is to say, the assumption that nationalism has only one objective, shuts out the investigation of different nationalist perspectives in terms of the classes which support them and their content.

The necessity for transcending one-dimensional views of class and race and the relationship between them has been dramatised by the changed conditions in South Africa since the Soweto uprisings in 1976 which were discussed in Chapter 1 in the course of the critique of a version of the notion of historical continuity, and in Chapter 2 in the analysis of the shift from economic determinism, in liberal modernisation theory, to a reformist interventionism in the political sphere by corporate capital. There the point under discussion concerned the reasons for this shift, but those changes have also provoked the need to investigate old questions about race and class in a new context. In particular, two changes were outlined: the relative decline in the need for cheap black labour and the increasing costs of maintaining stability in the face of black opposition.

Whether or not, in the long run, capitalism left to its own devices would dissolve white domination as liberal modernisation theory argues (the theory cannot be refuted as it always postulates a future event), has become irrelevant because for certain major white economic and political forces, the two changes have made political intervention in opposition to, and for the dismantling of, apartheid a necessity. For them, the promise of a slow, evolutionary transformation inspired by economic forces is no longer enough. Their purpose now is, precisely, to create the political space in which the rationality of the free market system can operate, that is to say, to ensure the reproduction of capitalism under new conditions.

What this means is that opposition to white domination has become coupled with a policy, the objective of which is to ensure the prolongation of capitalism. Furthermore, this objective finds support from the small black bourgeoisie and the growing black petite bourgeoisie within 'white' South Africa and from these same classes inside the bantustans, particularly the 'bureaucratic' bourgeoisie in control of the subordinate state apparatuses in those territories.

This recognition, that the relationship between capitalism and white domination is historically contingent, is the necessary starting point for a re-conceptualisation of race and class which will permit the theoretical closures discussed above to be overcome.

The relevance of this to the trajectory of political conflict and, in particular, to the analysis of rifts and alliances between the major social forces, is plain. In the discussion which follows the object is to formulate the concepts of class and race in a way which will open up the analysis of the inter-penetration of these phenomena in South African society.

## A NON-REDUCTIONIST CONCEPT OF CLASS

There is, of course, nothing novel in the quest for a non-reductionist theory of class within Marxism. The debate on this issue has been of profound significance because theoretical conclusions have informed political perspectives with fateful results. It is not intended in this section to traverse the literature on this subject which begins with Marx's own political writings. Rather, my object is to intervene in the debate keeping very much in mind the specifically South African literature and the difficulties which have been placed in the way of conceptual clarity by intricacies of the race and class divisions in the society. In the exposition which follows, in the attempt to contribute to a conceptual clarification, I draw generally on the extensive Marxist literature and particularly on the highly theoretical interventions of a variety of writers in recent years. [1]

In Chapter 1, it was suggested that, from a Marxist standpoint, the indispensable starting point for an analysis of a capitalist social formation was the concept of capital accumulation and the corresponding concept of the relations between capital and labour. The reason is that these concepts define the relations which demarcate a field of investigation different from that which may be delineated by other theoretical approaches. It was implied, however, that the concept of class which establishes the essential, but limited, economic nexus between capital and labour, cannot be construed as also entailing other qualities (ideological and political positions, culture and so forth); that is to say, the *concept* of class is not also simultaneously an empirical description of concrete classes and the *concept* does not contain a prediction of the concrete, empirical consequences which *will* follow irrespective of other conditions. To the contrary, the concept is abstract in the sense that it does not include in its terms either non-economic or, indeed, concrete economic conditions. To repeat, it demarcates an essential but incomplete field of relations.

At the abstract level, both capital and labour are, necessarily, conceptualised as unitary and homogeneous classes and the relation between them as an undifferentiated relation of exploitation. This is so because the concept specifies what the common property is of each class – fundamentally ownership of capital (means of production) on the one side and non-ownership on the other side – and the definition of an historically specific but general relation of exploitation, that is, the extraction of surplus value. It is precisely for this reason that the abstract concept does not provide a *sufficient* basis for analysis. For, in this formulation, the concept does not recognise differentiation: departments of production, various and differentiated labour forces and capitals and different methods of production, the manual/mental division, gender and racial divisions and others.

The problem of reductionist Marxism, thus, is not its starting point, but the path it follows from the abstract to the concrete, a path which leads it to impose the abstract on the concrete as if they were homologous. This inevitably gives rise to a conception of given, objective class interests. The interests of the unitary classes, it is supposed, derive directly and entirely from the abstract concept which defines their *common* properties – the concept of the place they occupy in the relations of production – but no significance is attached to properties which *differentiate* them internally. The common, 'given' interests are held to govern all social relations, including the ideological and political superstructure. At the level of the superstructure, economic interests take on an ideological and political form. The latter are generated by the economic relations and the economic interests they embody. Thus, to the extent that conflicts in the political and ideological superstructure focus on race relations, these are nothing other than the (mystified) form of the economic class struggle determined by the clash of economic interests.

What this view fails to recognise is that while, at one level, classes may be conceived of as unitary entities, concretely, to the contrary, their internal unity is always problematic. Thus, in the economy itself, that is in the sphere of production and exchange, classes exist in forms which are fragmented and fractured in numerous ways, not only by the division of labour and, indeed, the concrete organisation of the entire system of production and distribution through which classes are necessarily formed, but by politics, culture, and ideology within that division of labour, for example, gender, religion, the mental-manual divide and racial differentiation. Classes, that is, are constituted, not as unified social forces, but as patchworks or segments which are differentiated and divided on a variety of bases and by varied processes. It is true that a more or less extensive unity may be brought about politically through the articulation, within a common discourse, of specific interests which are linked to the common property which defines the class. But, and this is the fundamental point, that unity is not given by the concepts of labour-power and capital, it is constituted concretely through practices, discourse and organisations. One might say that class unity, when it occurs, is a conjunctural phenomenon.

One important point which emerges relates to the meaning to be given to the notions of class conflict and class consciousness. In the literature, class consciousness and conflict are said to exist when 'class issues' are involved. But what are class issues? If classes are defined as economic entities, then class issues, it seems, must relate directly to the economic elements that define classes – presumably, the relations of production, wages and the like. Therefore, from this standpoint, class consciousness and class conflict can only be, in some sense, purely economic. Thus, race must be excluded from and opposed to class.

If, by contrast, it is accepted that classes are concretely formed, even in the sphere of production, simultaneously through politics, economics and ideology, then race may well become the content, under specific conditions, of the class struggle. As Stuart Hall (1982) has observed:

> Race is, thus, the modality ... in which class is 'lived', the medium through which class relations are experienced, the form in which it is appropriated and 'fought through' ... (p.341)

It follows from the above argument that the simple opposition between race and class in explaining South African history must be rejected. Race may, under determinate conditions, become interiorised in class struggles in both the sphere of the economy as well as the sphere of politics.

This conceptualisation allows us to formulate, at the concrete level, an alternative non-economistic conception of the economy and permits a more satisfactory understanding of the class content of the political struggles to end or sustain white domination in South Africa.

I have already, briefly, referred to the changed position of certain fractions of capital and I will return to this and related issues in the final chapter. Here, I want to remark on the political position of the black petite-bourgeoisie and the black working-class. A caveat is necessary because in the present, extremely rapidly changing, conjuncture, any account of the political strategy and outlook of classes and class fractions is likely to be out of date by the time these words are published. Nonetheless, the discussion which follows remains pertinent to the issue being addressed, that is, the question of the way in which the class and national liberation struggles articulate, because it problematises the assumption that opposition to white domination will necessarily function to unite all black classes against the regime. It opens the possibility that opposition to racial domination *may* tend to unite black people across class lines and, yet, specifically defined class interests may at the same time tend to divide them along class lines. Similarly, investment in white domination may tend to unite white people across class lines and yet, at the same time, specifically defined class interests may tend to divide them. Which tendency will 'triumph' will depend on the conjuncture; it is not given by either the class or the racial structure. This, in fact, is the question of the class content of the national liberation struggle.

The examples which follow are intended to highlight, on the one hand, the way in which the class interests of the black petite-bourgeoisie have tended to divide this class from the black working-class; and, on the other hand, the way in which divisions may occur within a single black class, the working class. The point is to illustrate the varying content of opposition to white domination.

In recent years, partly as a result of the South African regime's bantustan policies and partly because of the enormous expansion of the home consumer market, there has been a considerable growth of a black petit-bourgeosie which has become increasingly organised both through economic enterprises (for example, the African Bank) and through organisations such as the National African Chamber of Commerce as well as through the bantustan political apparatuses.

The black petite-bourgeoisie is opposed to white domination but despite the very different conditions of their formation, both sectors (urban and bantustan) are dependent on the apartheid state for their development, however limited that may be. The bantustan petite-bourgeoisie owes its creation and its expansion and reproduction to the political institutions of the bantustans. In this respect the bantustan development plans, and indeed, the entire decentralisation policies of the state have led to the emergence of a class of large and medium sized land-owners. In Kwazulu and the Transkei (as in other bantustans) the formation of a class of commercial farmers has been effected through preferential access to credit, marketing boards and irrigation schemes, This petite-bourgeoisie (and, to a much smaller extent, the bourgeoisie) has a vested interest in the bantustans no matter how much it may demand consolidation of land or raise objections to other features of the contemporary situation.

In the case of the urban black petite-bourgeoisie, it cannot be assumed that changes in government policies, which have brought it some advancement, will automatically ensure its co-operation with the regime. But neither does the fact that the structures of racial domination continue to operate in respect of this class while economic restraints are eased, guarantee that it will move towards the liberation movement. Indeed, its response may be to press vigorously its own narrow economic interests while collaborating politically with the regime – the participation of members of this class in the black urban councils is a case in point. That is, a part of the petite-bourgeoisie may see its salvation, not in a political alliance with the African National Congress for the revolutionary overthrow of the apartheid regime, but rather through economic struggles to eliminate racial impediments to their own self-expansion. It is this possibility which opens the way for an alignment of this class with corporate capital's reformist strategy leading, if successful, to a de-racialised form of capitalism.

It was pointed out earlier that the African National Congress regards the working class as the leading force in the struggle to establish a national democratic state, yet the recent recognition of black trade unions by the state has had effects which made, and still make, this, at least in the short term, an uneven process. Thus, at one point a split developed among the unions: one section, including the Federation of South African Trade Unions or, at least, its leadership, argued that the unions must stand apart from the nationalist political struggle (as conducted, for example, by the United Democratic Front) for the implementation of the Freedom Charter. Instead, it was contended, the unions must utilise their new legality to win better wages and conditions for the workers in the factories – indeed, to ally themselves with the political struggle would be to endanger their existence because of likely repressive state intervention.

The force of these brief examples is twofold. Firstly, they challenge the view that the emergence and reproduction of racial orders can be analysed in isolation from their location in the economic and political system. Secondly, it challenges the attempt to analyse political conflicts in a manner which simply assumes the homogeneity of the racial entities and, indeed, of the policies and practices which are pursued within and in relation to them.


ECONOMIC AND POLITICAL STRUCTURES

Thus far, the focus in this chapter has been on the inter-penetration of race and class in terms of the *concerns* of classes or class fractions. It is clear, however, that, the argument that racial *concerns* may become interiorised within class concerns, does not completely dispose of the problem of economism. Nor, moreover, given the theoretical position adopted in this book, does the pre-occupation with *concerns* provide a sufficient basis for defining the specificity of the political sphere. These two aspects are connected for, it is contended, the relative autonomy of the political from the economic depends on their structural differentiation. This returns us to the question of the structure or the morphology of the economic and, in particular, of the political sphere.

It must be recognised from the outset that, while the struggles (the 'concerns') within the political system and the economy may, indeed, be different and clearly distinguishable, although not necessarily unconnected, at least in the sense that they may have effects on one another, however indirect these may be, it is also the case that the objective of struggles within these different spheres may coincide. Nonetheless, whether the concerns are or are not routinely different, what demarcates economic from political concerns is that they are mediated by distinct institutional and organisational matrices which structure their form and, in large measure, their content. Burawoy (1985) has formulated the point in the following way:

> ... we must choose between politics defined as struggles regulated by *specific apparatuses*, politics defined as struggles over *certain relations*, and the combination of the two. In the first, politics would have no fixed objective, and in the second it would have no fixed institutional locus. I have therefore opted for the more restrictive third definition according to which politics refers to struggles within a specific arena aimed at a specific set of relations. (p.253–4)

In the political sphere, state apparatuses and the relations between them (for example, judiciary, executive and legislature), the organisation of political parties and so on, structure the mode and content of struggles for state power. By contrast, in the sphere of production, the apparatuses of management, trade union organisations, the institutions of industrial relations, the organisation of the labour process and the like structure class struggles over the relations of and in production.

Burawoy's formulation is, however, too restrictive for the objectives of struggle in the two spheres (as was suggested in the discussion of Nolutshungu) may not be as clearly segregated as he suggests. Thus, for example, in the political sphere one objective may be to impose a specific, racialised division of labour in productive enterprises; on the other hand, struggles in the enterprises may be directed to the political sphere precisely in order to win the political conditions for the abolition of racial practices in production. The crucial point is that in either case the structure of each sphere will condition the form and orientate the content of the struggles which occur.

This formulation enables us to raise again the question concerning the effects of the relationship between the sphere of production (or more generally the economy) and the political sphere on racialisation or de-racialisation in either arena. Once we abandon the iron law of economic reductionism it is possible, as I showed above, to recognise that the relations between the sphere of production and the sphere of politics may be complementary, contradictory or both.

It can be shown that over a long period in the development of capitalism in South Africa, the structures of racial domination in the political sphere provided a legal framework and coercive state apparatuses for the imposition of racial structures and practices within production. Racialisation in one sphere became the condition for the same process to occur in another sphere. The establishment of administrative structures over already existing and spatially separated pre-colonial communities, the subordination of indigenous law, politics and culture and so on, provided the political, ideological and legal foundation for the racial positioning of subjects in the arena of production as capitalist production developed. In recent years, a restructuring of the division of labour, rapid upward mobility of white labour, the struggles of the black workers in the factories and outside, and other changes have begun, in part, to erode the dominant and monolithic character of racial categorisations in the economy. One effect of this has been to set up pressures for changes in the political sphere. So far, these pressures have been resisted although in one or two respects – recognition of black trade unions, abolition of job reservation – the polity has yielded; in other respects – the tri-cameral parliament, urban black representation – the form has been altered, but the imposition of racial categorisations continues.

The relations which become the object of contestation and the mode in which that contest is conducted will be mediated by the particular institutional and organisational structure within the different spheres of the society. At the same time, the relations in one arena may become the object of struggle in the other although the form of struggle will be conditioned by the specific institutional and organisational matrices of the latter.

The point can be illustrated by an example drawn from the recent debate about the registration of black trade unions. This issue has long since been resolved but, through it, the importance of not neglecting the structural conditions can be demonstrated.

Central to that debate was the question of the effects the law governing the registration of black trade unions might have on the character and functional capacity of the unions if they registered. The fear of the unions opposed to registration was that the law would operate to undermine their democratic organisation and bureaucratise them and, in the process, separate them from the general movement for national liberation. The pro-registration position was that the rights contained in the law had to be exploited in the interests of the workers and to establish, under the protection of the law, strong unions even if this meant restricting the activities of the unions to shop floor struggles. Insofar as the law might bureaucratise or otherwise affect the unions, the workers' struggle would serve to offset such possibilities.

The theoretical issue which underlay the dispute, then, was: in what sense can the law be said to have effectivity and yet, at the same time, be within the realm of, and made vulnerable to, class struggle? What are the theoretical tools needed to answer this question? If, whatever the provisions of the law, it is *always* and unconditionally vulnerable in its operation to oppositional struggles, then the law, as such, loses all significance. If, however, the law is one of the conditions of struggle, in the sense that its provisions are relevant to the definition of both the terms and the mode of struggle, then it is impossible *simply* to invoke the role of struggle. It goes without saying that I am dealing with a situation in which the regime still has under its control the coercive and other apparatuses of the law. Obviously, there may well be conditions, short of revolutionary transformation, in which the law is rendered, at least partially, inoperative – the situation of dual power is, perhaps, one such instance. In the type of situation I am concerned with, detailed attention must be paid to the provisions of the law and the specificty of its constraining effects.

The argument is that the the specific terms of the law and the form of state apparatuses may serve to structure the form, content and organisation of the class struggle. This, of course, is not to argue that the mode of operation of the law will remain unaffected by the struggle. The purpose is not to lay down ahistorical, universal statements, but rather to argue that where an institutional order has been established as the outcome of class and other struggles, then that order (with all its supports through state and other apparatuses) will have an extremely important effect on the definition of the space and parameters of struggle. The argument can be illustrated through the notion of 'access'.

I have argued elsewhere (Wolpe, 1980; 1985) that certain state apparatuses provide the possibility for mass or class struggles and others do not. The difference lies in the type of access which is available in relation to different state apparatuses. This means that the form of the struggle will vary according to the content of the law.

There are at least two different modes of access to state apparatus which may have vastly different effects upon the possibilities of class struggle from within these apparatuses. In one case 'access' may function to isolate individual subjects from one another and hence tend to individualise conflicts. It is here that Poulantzas's (1973) notion of the isolation effect of the state and law has applicability. For example, the arraignment of an individual in courts, or his or her registration in a labour bureau may give 'access' to the state but it does so in a mode which, while it brings the individual into an 'external' relationship with the administrative or judicial apparatuses, precludes, within the sphere of the apparatus, the formation of relations between the subjects themselves. The effect of both these features is to impose strict limits on the possibility of political struggles from within the state structures. Of course, the court may, nonetheless, become an element in struggles outside of the state apparatus as when the political organisations raise demands about the fate of the accused and the operation of the law. But, in this case, the arrangements established through state and law determine the limits and resistance must take the form of general political campaigns, including mass defiance of the law organised from outside the institutional order in question.

By contrast, access to such apparatuses as state schools and legislative assemblies, which are premised on, and depend on, access of individual subjects or representatives who are brought into direct relationship with one another, provide different conditions of action. Here, the law does not have an 'isolating' effect; on the contrary it makes participation a *sine qua non* of the functioning of the institution and thus establishes an essential condition for the possibility of a politics of participation within such state apparatuses. [2] In sum, the concrete nature of struggles over state and law are conditioned by the specificity of the institutional structure of the state and the content of the law.

CONCLUSION

In this chapter two separate but related arguments were advanced. The first attempted, by distinguishing between abstract and concrete conceptions of class, to establish the theoretical basis for the contention that class and race were not to be considered as phenomena which were necessarily external and opposed to one another. It was shown that considerations of race may become interiorised in class demands. At the same time, this provides the basis for recognising that both race and class are mutually implicated in the formation of demands which may stress racial as against class issues and vice versa.

The second argument, in essence, advances non-reductionist conceptions of the economy. Once it is accepted that racial considerations enter into the structuring of class relations, and that class relations influence the structure of the racial order, then it is no longer possible to distinguish between race and class on the basis that the former is an exclusively political phenomenon and the latter an exclusively economic one. Nor is it tenable to differentiate the economy from the polity in terms of the demands or concerns advanced in each sphere even if certain issues may tend to arise routinely in each sphere. The basis for differentiating political from economic struggles and processes is through the mediating effect of the institutional and organisational structure which is specific to each sphere.

With these remarks it is now possible to turn to a concrete analysis of contemporary South Africa. The theoretical analysis in this and the earlier chapters has explicitly argued, against the drift of the existing literature, that there is a contingent and, therefore, historically specific relationship between the capitalist and racial order. The uncoupling of this relationship also permits the recognition of the variant class content of policies which oppose racial domination. This opens the way for a concrete analysis of contemporary struggles which is able to encompass the contradictory as well as the complementary relationship between and effects of different social processes. These struggles are analysed in Chapter 5.

However, the content and character of these struggles are not unconditional. They are shaped by a structural order which, although itself the outcome of past conflicts, and vulnerable to present struggles, nonetheless sets the stage. The next chapter sets out to provide an account of the emergence of the structural conditions which provide the context for the analysis of the present conjuncture which is the subject matter of Chapter 5.

# 4 The Periodisation of the Apartheid Political System

In the previous chapters it has been argued that a simple conception of historical continuity has hindered the analysis of the political system in South Africa particularly during the apartheid era.

That capitalism and white domination, which owe their origins to the colonial period, continued to be reproduced after 1948, is beyond dispute. What is in contention, however, is the character of that reproduction. The simplified notion of continuity subordinates diversity to identity and in so doing assumes that the structure of racial domination is constituted as a fully integrated, monolithic, and homogeneous unity that is neither subject to uneven development nor riven by contradiction but remains in an unchanging relationship with the capitalist economy.

There are two implicit aspects of this position. The first is that, given the virtually exclusive *analytical* pre-occupation with white domination in much of the literature, the institutional structure of the social formation tends to be presented in a one-dimensional manner, as if the dimension of racial repression exhausts what is significant. This is, of course, not to deny the importance of the racially repressive character of the institutional order. But it is crucial to recognise that the modes of control and effects of white domination vary according to the specific institutions or apparatuses within which they operate. Moreover, these are linked in a matrix of relations which are complementary and contradictory both within and between the political and economic spheres.

The second aspect is that the social formation is presented as a seamless web of struggles – class, race or a combination of both. The result is that the structural conditions in which the conflicts take shape are de-emphasized and instead a descriptive account of the issues in contention, and of the course that the conflicts take, is provided. The outcome of the conflicts is then frequently attributed, vaguely and tautologically, to the fact that one side or the other held the balance of power.

Thus, as I pointed out in Chapter 3, the class struggle alone, according to Davis and Bob Fine, will determine the specific effectivity or otherwise of the law – the structure of the law itself, including its institutional supports, is accorded no significance. That political struggle is a powerful motive force of history is unquestionable but merely to leave it at that is insufficient. Instead, it is necessary to ask: what are the structural conditions under which specific issues become the object of contestation, how do these affect the organisation and mode of struggle and how do they contribute to the capacities of the contending forces?

It is, of course, possible and, indeed, analytically necessary to describe different phases of conflict, but to do so without reference to changes in the structural conditions is to omit from the account a crucial component of the explanation of those phases. The neglect of structural diversity tends to give an impression of underlying structural continuity. By coupling phases of struggle with structural diversity, on the other hand, the idea of historical discontinuity is captured without, however, abandoning a differentiated concept of continuity. As argued in Chapter 1, the notion of the general continuity of white domination and capitalism must be coupled with an analysis of the discontinuities, that is of the structural diversities which condition the conjunctural struggles. The analysis of discontinuities within continuity is encompassed within the concept of periodisation which should be construed in a way which itself encompasses the possibility of continuity within one sphere of the social and economic order with discontinuity in another.

Three phases or periods (perhaps, four, in the light of the transformations occuring at the time of writing) of the apartheid political system can be identified. Each of these is characterised by specific political and economic structural conditions and struggles. The existence of the structural conditions can be explained by the changes and struggles which occurred under the conditions of the preceding period.

In this regard, Davis and Bob Fine (1985) have commented:

> The periodization model reflects rather than explores the rigid separations which were in fact established [by the liberation movement – H.W.] between the periods of legal and illegal struggles. Here lies its limits. It reinforces what we might call a 'sequential exclusivism', according to which legal methods are reserved for one period and violent methods for another. It rules out a more fluid conception of their inter-connections, until that is, the arrival of a further period capable of synthesising them. (p.30)

The alternative to 'sequential exclusivism', for Davis and Fine, is clearly 'sequential non-exclusivism'. Their contention, that is to say, is that at all times 'a wider set of options' is available. Which option is, in fact, selected requires explanation and that explanation they find in the character of the political movement. [1]

Obviously, in principle, multiple choices are always available and, indeed, everywhere organisations on the same side of the political spectrum not only clash over which strategies should be selected, they actually operate by different strategies. But this is hardly the point; what is at stake is an analysis of the conditions which make one strategy rather than another plausible. That issue, undoubtedly, cannot be resolved merely by examining the character of the political movements. It requires a complex analysis of the social forces involved and the structural conditions within which the contests between them are occurring. The task cannot be undertaken here; instead, in what follows my object is more modest. It is primarily, to demarcate, in summary form, the character of the political phases of apartheid and to identify, however briefly, the causes which brought these phases into existence.

## 1948–1960: THE DECLINE OF THE STRUCTURAL CONDITIONS OF MASS STRUGGLE

When the National Party was elected to power by an all-white electorate (minor exceptions apart) in 1948, the institutions of white economic and political domination were, of course, already in place.

To begin with, the political/legal system defined a category of white subjects endowed with electoral rights on the 'Westminster-model' parliamentary system and in local and provincial government, economic rights in the ownership of land and other productive property, monopoly rights to certain occupations, and social rights to specific types of education and training, library and cultural facilities and much else.

It also defined various categories of black subjects. That definition was a condition of exclusion from many of the major political and economic institutions and resources available to white subjects including the right to vote, membership of parliament, provincial and municipal councils, land ownership (outside of the reserves), posts in the judiciary and skilled jobs. Where exclusion was not total, as in the case, for example, of the limited African communal and coloured franchise in parliamentary elections, access to the terrain of extra-parliamentary politics and organisations and trade unions in certain industries, participation carried with it constraints which did not apply to white subjects.

At the same time, legal definitions of the black subject constituted a condition of participation in two other categories of institutions and apparatuses. Firstly, in segregated, weak and extremely limited bodies such as, for example, the advisory boards in the black townships and the Native Representative Council which had only advisory powers. Secondly, as subordinated subjects in an array of structures of control and regulation – labour bureaux, pass laws, segregated townships and so on.

White domination and black subordination were, then, embedded in a particular political/economic institutional and organisational form and sustained by coercive, political and ideological apparatuses in all spheres, supported by an alliance of white social forces.

It is clear that race is inscribed in the institutional and organisational structures at every level of the political and economic system. Race is, thus, a crucial ingredient of the political and economic structure but, as has been argued throughout, it by no means exhausts the account of what is significant to the functioning of those structures.

At the level of the political system, it is necessary to stress again, firstly, the existence of a parliamentary system (comprising the legislature, the executive and its apparatuses and the judiciary) which has both a racially exclusive formation and its own logic of relations which, in its operation, has effects which cut across racial divisions; secondly, the existence of a sphere of extra-parliamentary politics. This leads us to consider the mode of functioning of, and relationship between, these components of the political system.

At the beginning of the apartheid period in 1948, the executive of the state – the cabinet, the civil service and the coercive apparatuses, including the security forces – was generally under the control of and responsible to the legislature.

At the same time, the judiciary enjoyed a considerable degree of autonomy from both the legislature and executive/bureaucratic arms of the state. That relation was expressed in a number of different ways of which the following are illustrative: judgments in favour of the individual against the actions of administrative authorities, for example, in cases of exclusion from housing by the superintendents of black residential townships and of declarations of vagrancy and expulsion from the urban area; judgments routinely interpreting the law so as to interfere least with the rights of the individual subject, including black subjects; judgments restraining the executive through habeas corpus orders; insistence upon conformity to the rules of natural justice.

The extent of the judiciary's power and autonomy from other state structures was also signalled, in the 1950s, in judgments of the Appellate Division, declaring legislation which attempted to deprive coloured people of the right to vote in parliamentary elections on the common voters' roll, to be unconstitutional. This right had been 'entrenched' in the South Africa Act 1909 by means of a procedural clause which laid down that a two-thirds majority, of both houses of parliament sitting together, was required to amend the voting section. The basis of the judgments was that, in passing the Acts, the legislature had failed to comply with the entrenched clause procedure, laid down in the South Africa Act. Indicative, too, was the refusal of the courts to accede to the application of the Law Society, the statutory professional body, that a black lawyer (Nelson Mandela), convicted of sedition, should be disbarred because he had been found guilty of disgraceful conduct rendering him unfit to practice as a lawyer. The Supreme Court held, however, that the actions for which he had been found guilty by the trial court,were undertaken for a legitimate cause, namely the economic and political advancement of the black people and that this was not a ground on which he could be disbarred.

Obviously, this is not to suggest that the judiciary had an unblemished record of asserting itself in all cases against the state and in favour of individual rights, or that judges did not give effect to the body of laws which were legal instruments of white domination in a capitalist social formation. Clearly, the overwhelming preponderance of legal judgments implemented the laws which reproduced this system.

Indeed, the judiciary in the existing legal space, at times, exercised a certain independence and at other times it did not. This suggests that what is important, then, is not only the individual decisions of individual judges – these are never entirely consistent in judiciaries with any degree of autonomy. If attention is focused entirely on judicial decisions, then the tendency is to reduce the explanation of judicial autonomy or subordination exclusively to the presence or absence of liberal judges (see, for example Sachs, 1973). It is worth noting in passing that in the 1950s many liberal judges, construing the law in the most judicial manner, did not consistently exert the court's autonomy by upholding the rights of the individual against state authority; by contrast, the most illiberal judges frequently did!

What is at issue, then, is not merely the inventory of judicial decisions, but also the extent to which the structure of the legal space, within a given social formation, gives room for judgments which control and limit the powers of other state institutions. In 1948, there existed, to a degree, such a legal space defined by strongly held ideologies about the independent role of the judiciary, by statutory guarantees of judicial autonomy, by the provisions of substantive criminal law which asserted or assumed the discretionary power of judges, particularly in relation to political acts, by legal precedents and, however imperfectly, by the practices of law enforcement agencies. [2] From 1948, that space began to be closed down through processes and under conditions which will be discussed below.

Thus far the concern in this chapter has been with the structures of the state as they existed when the National Party came to power. At that time, the political terrain outside of the state apparatuses was also structured in a way which gave room for the formation and activities of organisations and enterprises (for example, newspapers) which were, to varying degrees, radically opposed to the existing system. Although, within the Union of South Africa, the structure of civil society was characterised by an articulation of oppositional organisations, for example, the ANC [formed in 1912], black trade unions [among others, the ICU formed in 1919], the Communist Party [formed in 1921]; yet this structure was deepened under the conditions which developed during the years of the Second World War.

The flow of black migrants from the rural to the urban industrial areas was spurred by the industrial growth occasioned by the Second World War which increased the demand for labour and by declining living standards in the African rural reserves. Urban living conditions deteriorated rapidly and this was a crucial factor leading to squatters' illegal occupation of residential space in the townships, bus boycotts and other mass actions. A significant proportion of black industrial workers were organised in trade unions. This was accompanied by moves to build up and radicalise existing mass organisations such as the ANC and the Indian Congresses and to create an alliance between various organisations struggling for democratic rights. The regime's response, while not exactly welcoming, was also not entirely repressive, enmeshed as it was in the Second World War to 'preserve' democracy and eradicate racism. Thus, by the time the National Party was elected in 1948 there already existed a range of deeply-rooted extra-parliamentary, mass political organisations which were in the process of radicalising themselves and an organised trade union movement. Indeed, the electoral victory of the National Party was, at least in part, due to this radicalisation process and the failure of the South African Party government to curb it.

The increasing flow of black migration into the urban labour force came in part from white farms and in part represented a diversion of migrant workers from employment on the gold mines. The higher wage in manufacturing exerted a pull on black labour as against employment on the mines and the farms. On the one hand, the mines refused to increase wages, despite a sharp decline in the income of migrant families from rural production. On the other hand, the substantial failure of the state to implement the provisions of the Native Trust and Land Act of 1936 designed to force squatters on white farms into agricultural wage-labour, opened their way to migration on to the urban wage labour market. By the end of the war, the South African Party government was moving towards a policy which took cognisance of the interests of the fast growing manufacturing sector for a stable urbanised labour force and an expanded home market. This policy contemplated the partial ending of the migrant labour system and a reversal of the hitherto accepted principle that black workers were to be admitted to the urban areas only as temporary sojourners and only as long as they served the needs of the white population.

The government's policy, therefore, satisfied neither the mining industry nor the white farmers. Furthermore, white industrial workers felt threatened by the growth of a black industrial labour force whose presence could be utilised by employers to either lower their wages or undercut them with cheaper black labour.

The National Party came to power on a policy aimed at suppressing the emergent black opposition which threatened the reproduction of white domination, that is, threatened the conditions which would enable the regime to meet, inter alia, the demands of white farmers and protect the interests of the white working class. The interests of these classes were to be met by reversing the growing migration and permanent settlement of black workers in the urban areas. This meant restricting and strictly directing the movement of black labour by strengthening the system of influx control (labour bureaux and pass laws), meeting industrial needs with migrant labour and hence not developing the social conditions for a stable urbanised population and, finally, directing black labour to the white farms.

The draconian measures which the regime began to implement to give effect to these policies were, in large measure, an elaboration and modernisation of previously existing policies but, in the process, important structural transformations began to take place. In the present context, what is of significance is that these policies intensified the mobilisation of mass opposition and this, in turn, provoked the regime into introducing legislation and building its security apparatuses, which it utilised with increasing severity against the mass organisations. Behind these actions and counteractions profound structural changes were taking shape both within the state and in the political terrain.

Throughout the period between 1948 and 1960, precisely in response to the development of strong organisations of national liberation capable of organising powerful mass struggles, the government brought into operation a series of legal measures that had the effect of increasingly narrowing the space for legal political action. There is no need to dwell at length on these measures, which included the Suppression of Communism Act, which despite its title, empowered the arbitrary proscription of any organisation or individual who opposed the regime. Under this act the Communist Party and other organisations were banned, and hundreds of individuals were prohibited from attending meetings or belonging to political organisations or trade unions. The Public Safety Act provided for severe penalties for the commission of an offence, however trivial, by way of protest against state policies. Also the shifting of the burden of proof on to the accused in certain political trials; and the limitation of the discretion of judges in such cases.

At the same time the regime developed an elaborate structure of administrative control over the press and organisations and expanded the strength and powers of the security branch of the police force.

These processes had the effect of enhancing the power of the executive and, in particular, its coercive apparatuses, at the expense of the judiciary. As was noted earlier, this outcome was achieved by means of parliamentary legislation. The significance of this is that during the 1950s the authority of the judiciary over the executive precluded the latter from acting outside of the law and compelled it to seek legislative powers through Parliament. As was noted earlier, the supremacy of Parliament was the path by which the power of the executive was consitutionally increased and imposed over the legislature and the judiciary.

All this notwithstanding, and despite the extensive use of the coercive state apparatuses, the possibilities of mass mobilisation and political action existed. One important facilitating condition of this was, undoubtedly, the protection, albeit on a diminishing scale, offered by the law. Throughout the period a series of major campaigns against state policy were organised.

Davis and Bob Fine suggest that the above analysis is to be read to mean 'that a definite form of state determines the nature of the struggle from below' (1985, p.28). This is clearly to misunderstand the argument. It is not that the form of state is the single determinant of the nature of the struggle; rather, it is that the specific structure of the state is one, albeit extremely important, condition of the struggle. The form of the political sphere (not only the state but also the terrain of politics) is a determinant of the possible range of struggles – a political movement cannot, at will, simply launch any form of struggle irrespective of the form of the political system. In the 1950s a space for mass political mobilisation was present. This does not mean that other forms of struggle could not, or should not, have been undertaken; it also does not mean that all other forms of struggle were equally possible. It simply makes the point that struggles and structures must be understood in relation to one another.

To return to the main analysis, the situation described above contained the seeds of a crisis for the regime. On the one hand, the regime's policies generated intense, and continuous, opposition reflected in the growing involvement of the black masses in the national liberation struggles. On the other hand, it was incapable of subordinating and controlling the political opposition on the basis of its existing 'normal' powers, extensive as these were. Nor, despite numerous individual unlawful acts by the state, was the government, or the coercive state apparatuses, in a position to impose measures of control on a sufficient scale outside of the law. The ideology of the rule of law (in however an attenuated form) and the legal and other institutional constraints built into the existing state and political structures seemed to have ruled this out as an option, although why this should have been so still remains to be fully researched. The crisis erupted in March 1960 when an anti-pass demonstration at Sharpeville was broken up by the police with firearms; 69 people were killed, and some 200 more wounded. This event sparked strikes and demonstrations throughout the country. The regime wavered but then, to regain control of the situation, invoked the provisions of existing legislation to declare a state of emergency, arrested and imprisoned thousands of political activists, and called out the police and the army. The significance of Sharpeville, however, goes well beyond these immediate events.

## 1960–1973: STATE REPRESSION AND ARMED STRUGGLE

Firstly, Sharpeville provided the occasion for the state to utilise the Unlawful Organisations Act to declare the African National Congress and the Pan-Africanist Congress illegal organisations. It thus continued, on an expanded scale, the process of destruction of the extra-parliamentary political terrain, which began with the banning of the Communist Party in 1951 and was pursued in relation to various organisations throughout the 1950s. This, together with the use of emergency powers accelerated the restructuring of the political arena. It may be noted that a complementary processs was set in train in the Transkei, Western Transvaal and Zululand, where the crushing of peasant rebellions established the pre-conditions for the imposition of bantustan structures in these areas.

Although the emergency was lifted some six months later, its continuing impact was extremely powerful in a number of ways. Above all, it provided the regime with the instruments to control the exceptional upsurge in townward migration in the early 1960s which was a result of the economic boom which began in the late 1950s and which continued, on an expanded scale throughout the 1960s. The boom, which was stimulated by immense foreign investment especially following the political 'stability' imposed by the regime following Sharpeville, was particularly marked in the manufacturing sector. Between 1960 and 1970, the labour force in this sector increased by some 63%. Thus, despite the existing battery of influx controls and removal policies which the regime deployed, it was faced with a mounting flow of black migration to the urban areas. The emergency provided the model of control to meet this population pressure and any political threat arising from it.

The lesson for the regime came from its successful utilisation of a new method of political control – wide-ranging arbitrary powers which entirely precluded judicial intervention and which involved the massive deployment of the army and the police. The lesson for the national liberation movement was drawn from the very fact of the regime's co-ordinated use of these powers; it revealed how far the regime was prepared to go and thus put on the agenda the possibility of a turn to armed struggle. Despite this, the underground ANC and allied organisations organised a three-day stay-at-home in May 1961 and although there was large-scale police and army intervention during both the period of preparation and the strike itself, it was, at least, partially successful. Nevertheless, the national liberation organisations concluded that the cumulative effect of state action had so radically curtailed the already limited sphere of legal extra-parliamentary mass political action that it had no alternative but to forthwith institute a policy of sabotage with the intention of eventually developing an armed struggle against the regime. In *Strategy and Tactics of the ANC* (1969), it is stated:

> The general strike as a method of political mobilisation was suppressed with the utmost vigour and by the end of the fifties could no longer be effectively employed as an instrument of mass struggle. Other protests were increasingly broken by police brutality and the use of orthodox mass demonstration as an effective weapon was demonstrably not feasible. Legal opposition was rendered ineffective by bannings, exile and the imprisonment of activists and leaders to long terms for the most trivial infringements. Finally by such laws as the Terrorism and Sabotage Acts all opposition by legal or peaceful means was rendered impossible. (p.176)

This characterisation of the situation after the stay-at-home in May 1961, has been questioned by various writers. Davis and Bob Fine (p.44), for example, suggest that 'The evidence for a severe state crackdown on legal activity is strong, though it was not total' and they pose the question: 'Was it the case that "all opposition by legal or peaceful means" had been rendered impossible in 1961?' Before dealing with this question, it is necessary to draw attention to Davis and Fine's conflation of 'legal' with 'peaceful' for, clearly, it is perfectly possible to conduct illegal but peaceful political activities. And, indeed, that this was quite clearly the ANC's intention is demonstrated by the fact that it continued with illegal meetings, leaflet distributions and other work in the period immediately following the establishment of *Umkhonto We Siswe*, the military wing of the liberation movement. The importance of this is that it underlines the fact that, contrary to Davis and Fine's claim, the strategy of armed struggle was not seen as a substitute for work among the mass of the population.

Nonetheless, it is true that the most extreme measures of the state, the Terrorism and Sabotage Acts, were introduced *after* the turn to armed struggle. That is to say, it was the change of strategy of the national liberation movement that provoked a systematic response from the regime to block the threat to its existence which would be posed by an armed struggle.

The Terrorism and Sabotage Acts not only provided for extremely harsh penalties (including the death sentence) but also increased police powers, further limited the role of the judiciary, and placed a still heavier burden of proof on accused persons to establish their innocence in trials. The law also provided for periods of detention which could be repeated endlessly at the discretion of the police. In such instances, the courts' power to grant habeas corpus was abolished and the way opened for interrogation under torture. This was accompanied by a massive increase in the powers of the security forces and, indeed, the constitution of the security apparatus as the dominant arm of the state.

The fact that these measures followed the turn to armed struggle rather than preceding it means that the question posed by Davis and Bob Fine remains to be answered. Yet, right or wrong, once the decision was taken and the state responded as it did an entirely new situation was created. The outcome of the state's policies was not only the abolition of virtually all legal rights to extra-parliamentary political activity but, in addition, the substantial elimination of the organisations within this sphere by banning them and proscribing and imprisoning their activists. In this period (1960–1973), then, the terrain of extra-parliamentary mass political struggle was virtually abolished. The regime's success in this regard provided the untrammeled conditions for it to create all the instruments it required for the purpose of crushing the organisation of the armed struggle.

In this situation, the question of strategy had to be posed afresh. Slovo (1976) argues that:

> In South Africa in the early sixties the increasing concentration of the liberation movement on military preparation helped to generate an attitude both within the organisation and amongst the people that the fate of the struggle depended upon the sophisticated actions of a professional conspiratorial elite. The importance of the mass base was theoretically appreciated; but in practice mass political work was minimal. This attitude was to persist for some years after 1963 with propaganda tending to say too little about what initiatives people should be taking, and to treat them only as support groups for guerilla units which would soon appear amongst them. (p.193)

While it might have been the case that propaganda was mis-directed in the way Slovo suggests, this does not dispose of the issue of mass political work. The question of what work was possible and how it could be conducted relates not to the content of propaganda but to the possibilities of such work under extremely repressive conditions. In fact, the space for political campaigns and even illegal political work among the masses was virtually sealed off and this was a function not merely of state repression but also of the near destruction or emasculation of the major political organisations. For a period, the state had extraordinary control of the political sphere and little more was possible than sporadic acts of sabotage and illegal leaflet distributions.

This had far-reaching consequences not only for the form of struggle but also its content. The fact that the struggle assumed mainly the form of sabotage meant that there was little room for political campaigns around the sort of particular demands for reform that had been at the centre of the liberation struggles during the 1950s and which had been the basis of mass mobilisation; repeal of the pass laws, a living wage, the right to vote, the right to organise trade unions and to strike, the right to a good education, and so forth. What was now put in issue was state power, not as a comcomitant of intermediate, reformist demands (which, however, had revolutionary connotations), but directly through the instrumentality of the acts of underground units of the organisation.

## 1973–MID-1980s: THE RISE OF THE INSURRECTIONARY STRUGGLE

Although a full account of the 1960s has still to be written, it is nevertheless possible to point to profound changes which were occuring 'underneath' the repression and which opened the way for a transformation of the political sphere in the 1970s.

The political stability which was imposed by state repression in the 1960s laid the basis for large scale investment (particularly foreign investment) in the manufacturing industry in South Africa. The expansion of this sector took place on the basis of capital intensification. The familiar consequence was both the repulsion of labour into the pool of unemployed and the attraction of labour into the expanding economic sectors. One effect of this was to increase enormously the number of blacks unemployed. This 'surplus' labour force was banished to the bantustans. At the same time, particularly given the tendency for the white population to move out of manual occupations into white-collar, administrative and technocratic jobs (itself the result of economic expansion) there was a massive increase in the number of black workers recruited into industry. Furthermore, the pattern of employment shifted increasingly away from unskilled to semi-skilled work.

The growth of agri-business in white agriculture was also based upon capital intensification and involved the relative stabilisation and the further proletarianisation of the work force, coupled with the expulsion of hundreds of thousands of agricultural workers who were made to join the banished urban dwellers in the bantustans where, together, they formed a displaced and destitute population of approximately three million people.

An additional aspect of the economic 'boom' was the expansion of the tertiary sector again drawing in, to an unprecedented extent, black workers who had previously been more or less excluded from employment in that sector.

What was occurring, then, was the expansion of the black wage-labour force placed in a greater variety of occupations than ever before, acquiring greater skills, more stability and becoming increasingly important to employers as producers and as consumers of wage goods.

I earlier pointed out that capital intensification in industry had the important consequence that a sector of capital was becoming less interested in preserving the infrastructure of control which kept in place the system of cheap black migrant labour. For this sector, forming skilled personnel (given pressing shortages of skilled white workers) and labour stabilisation were more important as was the desire to institutionalise industrial relations and in that way end costly and disruptive 'wildcat' strike actions. In the economy, therefore, the restructuring of capital-labour relations was under way.

In a different sphere, in the black schools and universities, another development of momentous importance was taking place – the emergence of the black consciousness movement. Although the Bantu Education Act of 1953 was explicitly intended to instil compliance and passivity into the African youth together with a restricted form of elementary education, the schools provided the site for a quite different result. By the beginning of the 1970s the number of black students in (mainly) elementary schools had risen to 2.75 million from three-quarters of a million in 1953. By 1976 the number had risen to some 3.75 million.

In the conditions of repression in which mass political organisation and action was suppressed, politics retreated to the educational and cultural spheres. The concentration of large numbers of black youth in the schools and of increasing numbers of students in the recently established black universities provided a site, perhaps the only one in the repressive conditions of the time, in which a radical ideology (black consciousness) could develop. One reason for this was the relatively protected position of the educational institutions. The South African Students Organisation was formed in 1969 and the preamble to the constitution adopted in 1970 stated:

Whereas, we the Black students of South Africa, having examined and assesed the role of Black Students in the struggle for the emancipation of the Black people in South Africa and the betterment of their social, political and economic lot, and having unconditionally declared our lack of faith in the genuineness and capability of multi-racial organisations and individual Whites in the country to effect rapid social changes ... do commit ourselves *to the realisation of the worth of the Black man, the assertion of his human dignity and to promoting consciousness and self-reliance of the black community.* (Quoted in Hirson, 1979, p.72. *Emphasis added*)

By 1972, there was a shift towards political action on the part of the various black consciousness groups and a proliferation of demonstrations and other actions in the schools and universities.

The processes, briefly and superficially outlined above, culminated in two events which were to herald the reconstitution of the terrain of extra-parliamentary mass politics. The first of these events was the large-scale African workers' strikes in 1973. These strikes which involved some 60,000 workers, were, in part, the direct product of the important changes in the economy to which I referred at the beginning of this section. But they were also spurred by the conditions of economic crisis of the early 1970s.

The major features of this crisis were, firstly, a growing balance of payments deficit induced by the persistent need of manufacturing to import production machinery (given the undeveloped state of capital goods production in South Africa) and the decline in the price of gold. This was accompanied by a shortfall in investment capital required by manufacturing capital. Secondly, an acute shortage of skilled labour hampered the rate of mechanisation of the manufacturing industry and, thirdly, the capital intensification process had, itself, contributed to the massive growth of unemployment among blacks. The effect of the recession was to make employers particularly resistant to wage demands from black workers.

A number of factors present in 1973 made it more difficult for employers to crush the strikes even with the support of the state. These factors relate to the changed character of the black labour force: for example, the stabilisation of the work force, the increasing level of skills which were not, as before, easily replaceable by employers and, perhaps, higher levels of literacy due to the massification of education under the Bantu Education Act.

The strikes ushered in a period of intensive industrial unrest in all the major industrial areas and an unprecedented growth of an independent black trade union movement. This led to legislation permitting, for the first time, the legal recognition of African workers as 'employees' and the legal recognition and registration of African trade unions with the accompanying right – albeit under highly hedged conditions – to strike. [3]

In the wake of the industrial struggles, and, no doubt spurred by them, mass opposition to the policies and practices of apartheid, particularly as these affected everyday conditions of life, began to emerge under the influence of the black consciousness movement, in the black communities and schools. Militant action in the schools was fuelled by the reversal of the state's policy of expansion of secondary education for blacks – a reversal induced by the cut backs following the economic recession of the early 1970s. These conflicts culminated in the Soweto uprisings of 1976. The impact of Soweto on the political scene cannot be overemphasised because it established the fact that under changed conditions, mass political struggles had led to the restructuring of the political system – a change in the form of the state and the restoration, on new terms of the terrain of extra-parliamentary mass politicals. The character of these changes, which are briefly elaborated in the next chapter, are crucial to our understanding of the present conjuncture since, as I have tried to demonstrate for each period, the character and significance of struggles must be understood in terms of the relationship between the structural conditions and the form and content of those struggles.

# 5 The Present Conjuncture: the Prospects for Change

INTRODUCTION

In this chapter my object is to bring to bear the arguments, which have been advanced in the earlier chapters, on an analysis of the present conjuncture. I have not set out to write a detailed account of the contemporary situation, rather my purpose is to indicate in broad outline how the changes in the structural conditions of the political system and the shifting nexus between class and race and between racial domination and the capitalist economy, give shape to current struggles over the status quo.

The central thrust of the argument throughout the book has been that the level of commitment to, and the specific content of support for, as well as of opposition against, the racial order is by no means uniform or homogeneous within each racial group. Race and class may intertwine in variant and shifting ways. A single class, defined in terms of relations of production, may be deeply divided along racial lines when different sections, in mounting demands or protecting positions (for example, over access, to skills, wages, etc) invoke exclusionary racial discourses and practices. The schism between black and white in the working class in South Africa is an obvious case in point.

By contrast, fissures along class lines may occur within racially defined groups in which case the specific content of racial discourses and practices will vary according to the way they are incorporated by the different classes into their definition of interests. In this case, the relations between the same classes within different racial groups may vary from opposition and hostility to convergence and co-operation in which the political attachment to racial divisions is abandoned or, at least, becomes weakened. For example, in contemporary South Africa, there are common objectives in the policies of corporate capital and of sections of the black petite bourgeoisie and bourgeoisie.

Furthermore, the racial division of classes and the class division of races may be present simultaneously. This means that, on the one hand, cross-class alignments, in which there are differing attachments to the racial order, may co-exist and articulate with cross-race alignments in which attachments to the racial order are subject to dissolution. The question of the strength and weakness of these different relations at any moment is a matter for concrete analysis. Manifestly, therefore, it is not possible to read off group interests from either 'pure' race or class categorisations.

The implication of this is that particular combinations of race and class are not immutable. At one stage, the definition of interests may involve a convergence of race and class; at another, race and class may be perceived as contradictory. More broadly, as was argued earlier, the relationship between capitalism and white domination is an historically contingent, not a necessary, one. It follows that it cannot be assumed *a priori* either that the relationship is eternally contradictory or functional.

The view that racial domination is eternally functional for capitalism carries with it the argument that the 'needs' of the existing social formation or the interests of dominant classes 'cause' the structures and relations necessary for the satisfaction of these 'needs' and interests to be produced. That is, the 'needs' or interests generate the functions they require for their maintenance. This functionalist argument excludes both contradiction and the differentiated effects of conflict from its account. Contrastingly, liberal modernisation theory excludes functionality, but, at the same time, abolishes struggle – social transformation occurs, *deus ex machina*, in an evolutionary movement spurred by the economy. As against both these positions, two contentions have been advanced in this book: first, that the relationship between capitalism and the racial order is the contingent outcome of struggles between contending groups or classes and, secondly, that that outcome is always simultaneously functional and contradictory, advancing the interests of certain classes and, at the same time, undermining the interests of others and, moreover, securing the existence of certain structures and threatening that of others. Which pole of the relationship will be dominant depends on the historically specific conditions of the social formation.

In the next section, following the line of argument in Chapter 4 in which the relevance of a *structural periodisation* was emphasised, the characteristic of the political structure as it emerged in the post-1976 period is sketched out. This constitutes the basis for developing an analysis of the contemporary conjuncture in the remainder of the chapter.

THE RESTRUCTURING OF THE POLITICAL SPHERE

In the previous chapter, I described the repressive structure and the corresponding dominance of the coercive apparatuses and the coercive mode of functioning of the state in the 1960s. I also outlined, briefly, some of the changed conditions which made possible, and provoked, despite the form of the political system, the re-emergence of popular struggles on a sufficiently large scale and with sufficient continuity to bring about a reconstitution of the extra-parliamentary political arena. This was accompanied, at the same time, by a defensive and offensive restructuring of the state.

The point about these popular struggles is that they were neither sporadic nor confined to a narrow spectrum of issues. The starting points were, firstly, the strikes of black workers for higher wages in 1973 and, secondly, the student opposition to Afrikaans as a medium of instruction which resulted in the Soweto uprising in 1976. Very rapidly, broad sections of the black population (more particularly in the urban areas) were mobilised, on an unprecedented scale, around a wide spectrum of social, political and economic questions. Everything was put in issue – in the schools, the entire system of 'Bantu Education'; in the communities, segregation, health, housing, transport, the position of women, the pass laws, political rights; in the economy, jobs, wages, conditions of work and job reservation.

Although the struggles and the issues were frequently local and disparate, varied and diffuse, two factors were at work which tended to unite them at an ideological and policy level as well as organisationally. Firstly, they were occurring in a situation in which the ANC, which had re-emerged as the leading national liberation organisation, emphasised, particularly through the Freedom Charter (which was discussed in Chapter 2) the linkage between the specific demands of the separate struggles and their common solution in the elimination of the apartheid system. What is of great significance is that the discrete, specific reformist demands became linked together within the rubric of the Freedom Charter and its vision of a national democratic, socially and economically transformed society.

Secondly, regulation by the state of the conditions of life of the black people and their subordination in every sphere to the structures of white domination, served both to politicise all demands and to link them, no matter how apparently disparate, to the apartheid system as such. Furthermore, the repeated repressive response of the regime to virtually all popular demands tended to bring home to the different communities and organisations the common basis of their oppression in the existing society.

The unification process did not stop at the common acceptance of the Freedom Charter, but, most importantly, in terms of the reconstruction of the political terrain, also took on an organisational form.

The organisational reconstruction of mass political action first took place in separate spheres. These were: (i) the revival of existing, but more or less dormant, general political organisations such as the Transvaal Indian Congress; (ii) the politicisation of basically non-political organisations such as cultural, religious and sporting institutions and bodies (iii) the formation of new, and the revitalisation of already existing, community organisations, civic associations, organisations of students and women, and committees formed to pursue limited aims in the communities and (iv) new, independent, black trade unions many of which considered that they had a role in community as well as shop floor struggles.

The conditions which impelled the popular understanding of the common basis of oppression in each different sphere, were also the conditions which encouraged moves to establish organisational unity.

This was ultimately given expression to in the United Democratic Front (UDF), formed in 1983. The UDF brought together some 700 community, trade union, cultural, sporting, religious, student and political organisations, representing over two million members, in a common front based on the Freedom Charter. The UDF is, thus, a key organisational mechanism linking disparate bodies and demands into a coherent programme. As Collinge (1986) says:

> Within a year of its launch . . . the UDF posed a fundamental challenge to the legitimacy of the National Party 'reform' plan. It orchestrated election boycotts which left no doubt that the new tri-cameral parliament meant rule by white South Africa. . . At the same time, from mid-1984 increasing numbers of UDF affiliates began to participate in direct mass action. This arose in part from the rejection of the revamped black local authorities. This challenged not only the legitimacy of these institutions but their very existence. (p.248)

The UDF did not, and does not, incorporate the entire black opposition to the apartheid regime. At about the same time that the UDF was formed, the National Forum was also established through an initiative of the Azanian People's Organisation (AZAPO) somewhat rejuvenated by the release from Robben Island in 1983 of black consciousness activists. Both the National Forum and AZAPO owe their inspiration to the black consciousness movement. These organisations represent a minority tendency within the extra-parliamentary opposition to apartheid. The basis of their separation from the mainstream of the national liberation movement organised in the UDF, Congress of South African Trade Union (COSATU) and the ANC around the Freedom Charter rests on their opposition to the non-racial organisation and policies of the latter organisations.

The counterpart of the emergence and strengthening of the directly political organisations was the development of a powerful black trade union movement. As a result of the repression of the 1960s, the South

African Congress of Trade Unions (the trade union arm of the Congress Alliance) [1] was unable, even before it was outlawed, to operate effectively. The black trade unions which continued in existence confined their activities strictly to shop floor issues and steered well away from confrontation with the state or engagement with wider political issues relating to white domination. Following the 1973 strikes, new independent black trade unions came increasingly into existence. The unions, however, were divided over the crucial issue of the relationship between trade union and political struggles and, consequently, various trade union federations were formed. Following the Wiehahn and Riekert Commissions (1979), legislation was passed in 1979 legalising black trade unions and providing for their registration. This change in state policy both stimulated the growth of new trade unions and intensified divisions with the trade union movement. The question of the politics of the black trade unions became concentrated on the issue of registration under the new industrial relations legislation. Nevertheless, unity talks were set in train and by the end of 1985 unions with a membership of some 500,000 workers united in the COSATU. This unification took place on a policy which unequivocally acknowledged the link between the trade union and national liberation struggles. The Council of Unions of South African (CUSA) and the Azanian Congress of Trade Unions (AZACTU) refused to merge into COSATU but recent policy statements seem to bring these organisations closer together, despite the influence of black consciousness on the former two bodies.

The establishment of these political and trade union organisations amounted to the reconstitution of the extra-parliamentary political terrain which had been virtually abolished in the 1960s and set the scene for the continuous expansion and strengthening of that terrain. It is of great significance that this continued reconstruction occurred under conditions in which the coercive power of the state, far from diminishing, was considerably strengthened through the increasing centralisation and militarisation of the executive.

CENTRALISATION AND MILITARISATION OF THE EXECUTIVE

Earlier it was pointed out that, in the period after Sharpeville, the judiciary was increasingly subordinated to the executive which continuously strengthened its position in the state structures. Furthermore, reference was made to the increasingly dominant position of the security apparatuses within the executive. In the period after 1973, while the position of the judiciary became more ambiguous (this will be discussed below) there was an ever-increasing concentration of power in the military and security apparatuses within the highly centralised executive.

The process began, as O'Meara (1982) has shown, with changes in the internal structure of the ruling National Party. These changes, which reflected the outcome of contestations between conflicting interests within the Party, had the effect of weakening Party conference control over specific policy which then became the preserve of the leadership and, in particular, of the Cabinet. The simple device was to restrict the subject matter of conferences to general principles, leaving policy to the Cabinet.

The second step was to greatly weaken parliamentary control over the executive by assigning to the Cabinet and its various committees power over matters which were no longer brought within the purview of Parliament.

The setting up of the reconstituted President's Council as a result of the 1983 legislation took the process a stage further in a number of different ways. These were the allocation of power to the State President to appoint Minister's Councils for each of the houses of the tri-cameral parliament, to appoint the Cabinet and to nominate 25 members to the President's Council; the granting to the President's Council or the State President on the Council's advice, the power to decide on general affairs legislation where a majority is not achieved in each of the three houses; and the control, amounting to legislative power, given to the State President over 'Black Affairs'.

But most important has been the penetration of the military and the security forces into the state apparatuses, particularly the executive, which has accompanied the centralisation process.

Previously, while the military and security forces had a key role in the state, this role was, nonetheless, performed at the behest of an administration which was strictly civilian in its structure and composition. With Botha's accession to the leadership of the National Party in 1978, however, the army entered both into the coercive structures as well as into other structures of the state. The military has its place, therefore, not merely in the Defence Ministry and in the armed forces but in the President's Council, in the State Security Council and in other departments of the state including economic planning. Similarly the security police force has found its way into policy-making and administrative apparatuses of the state. What has been erected, that is, is a parliamentary regime with great power centralised in a militarised executive.

The entry and diffusion of the military into non-military state apparatuses, as much as the expansion and strengthening of the armed forces, indicated how seriously the regime took the threat presented to it by the popular and armed struggles internally, but it was equally connected to the importance it attached, in its overall strategy, to the subordination of the front line states. The armed forces have played a crucial role in both these areas as is demonstrated by its actions in

Namibia, intervention in Angola, and incursion into Mocambique, Botswana, Lesotho and Swaziland and by the major part it plays today in the control, with the police, of the black townships. The other aspect of this process relates to the absorption of the security apparatuses into the heart of the executive. Central to the National Security Management System which links the security forces directly into the administration of the society are the State Security Council and the Joint Management Committees.

The State Security Council is chaired by the State President and comprises senior ministers, senior military, police and intelligence personnel as well as the heads of the main departments of the civil service and senior planners. The breadth of the Council's involvement in state affairs is indicated by the wide-ranging responsibilities of its 15 committees. These include constitutional affairs, economic and cultural matters, community services as well as military, police and civil defence matters.

This is replicated at the regional level through the Joint Management Committees. There is a network of these committees almost all of which are chaired by members of the police or the military. They normally consist of about sixty members and their work is carried out by sub-committees. Their functioning is shrouded in mystery but it is clear that they are involved in security as well as many other matters. There are three committees: The GIK (Gesamentlike Intelligensie Kommittee) which is concerned to identify local security threats and to co-ordinate the appropriate organs of the state to meet these threats; SEMKOM (Staatkundige, Ekonomiese en Maatskaplike Kommittee) whose task it is to idenitfy conditions in the local community which contribute to the production of the 'revolutionary climate' and to recommend how these should be dealt with; thirdly, KOMKOM which is charged with propagating the 'achievements' of the authorities and of winning the population away from alternative structures such as the civic associations. Below these committees are a network of local committees which gather information for the Joint Management Committees and its sub-committees.

Given this continuous expansion of executive power and of the role of the military and security forces, the question which poses itself is *how the re-emergence and strengthening of the structures of the extra-parliamentary political terrain is to be explained?* A number of different conditions appear to be relevant.

EXPLAINING THE RECONSTITUTION OF THE POLITICAL TERRAIN

*The 'New' Black Working Class*
Attention has already been drawn to the fact that economic development during the 1960s was characterised by three principal

structural changes. Firstly, the vast expansion of two sectors of the economy – capital intensive manufacturing and the tertiary sector – both of which provided jobs, and led to insistent demands for stable, black semi-skilled and white-collar labour. Secondly, an enormous growth in the black urban wage-earning population. Related to this, thirdly, a massive growth in the black consumer market upon which the manufacturing sector depended for its expansion.

The significance of these structural changes became apparent in the 1970s when, with the ending of the economic boom of the 1960s, massive unemployment and sharply declining living standards were added to the already intolerable and oppressive conditions of life – poverty, forced removals, pass laws and so forth – with the result that the black urban working class was galvanised into action.

What the struggles of the 1970s revealed was that the black urban working class was qualitatively different to that of the 1950s and that sharp cleavages had developed within the white bloc. The socio-economic foundation of these phenomena will be discussed more fully in the next section which analyses the emerging class divisions within the white community, but since policy divisions within the white community manifested themselves specifically in response to the organised mass struggles in the factories and in the largely working class black urban communities, it is relevant, at this point, to draw briefly the contrast between the character of the black urban population in the 1950s/1960s and in the 1970s at this point.

In the former period, the black labour force was largely uneducated and unskilled, easily replaceable in the occupational structure from the reserve army of labour, particularly in the African reserves and hence vulnerable to expulsion by the state to those reserves in the event of strikes and, also, subject to intense repression, criminal prosecution and dismissal. The black working class of the 1970s was first of all better educated than previously, reflected not only in the massification of primary education, but also in the vast increase in secondary school students from about 25,000 in the mid-1950s to over 300,000 in the early 1970s. Secondly, it contained a considerable proportion of semi-skilled and, despite the governent's policy, stable urbanised workers. Therefore, it became less easily replaceable, particularly under conditions of labour shortages. Above all, its political formation took place in the relatively sheltered environment of the schools in which an oppositional ideological movement, particularly in the form of Black Consciousness, was growing in the late 1960s and early 1970s. To a certain extent, the generation of workers which began to enter the labour market in the early 1970s, had been exposed less to state repression than the older generation and were filtered through the political ferment occurring in the schools.

These conditions contributed to the production of a more politically defiant and resistant urban work force than in the 1960s and, indeed, than in the 1950s. It was largely these workers who came to play, and continue to play, a leading role in both the trade union field and in the communities in the present period. The first condition, then, which facilitated the revival of the extra-parliamentary political terrain was the capacity of the 'new' working class to withstand the coercive actions of the state. But this both occasioned, and was made possible by, pressures towards reforms which emanated from specific sections of the white community.

## Contradictions and Conflicts Within the White Community

It may be said that contradictory and complementary pressures within the white community in the 1970s, which were absent in the 1960s, constrained the freedom of the regime to stifle political opposition to apartheid in the way and to the extent that it had been able to do in the 1960s. This was a further reason why the popular organisations were able to embed themselves so deeply before the regime and state began to act under emergency powers in 1985–6 and again in 1986–7.

If these constraints operated to *limit* the freedom of the regime to curb opposition in the 'old way' – that is by preventing the development of or destroying its organisational base – it encouraged it to attempt to control and limit radical opposition in other ways. The reconstruction of the political terrain not only gave rise to a new threat, on a vastly expanded scale to the apartheid system, it also produced counter initiatives by the regime to control that terrain. These involved a restructuring of the state and its policies in what has been termed a reformist direction. This response to the popular movement was connected to the emergence of pressures within the white community for the reform, even the abandonment of the apartheid system, which, in turn, was related to developments in class formation and related changing definitions of class interests.

## The Changing Class Formation Within the White Bloc

At different points in earlier chapters the argument that class and race and the capitalist economy and white domination stand in a contingent relationship to one another has been strongly advanced. I now want to use that insight to analyse how altered conditions have resulted in the reformulation of interests by various classes resulting in conflicts between a reformist tendency and a continued firm attachment to the reproduction of white domination more or less in its existing form.

Historically, in South Africa, the functional role of the racial order, for capitalism and for classes within the white community, was predominant despite the fact that it also had contradictory negative effects. To begin with it provided the conditions of reproduction of a cheap black labour force and, therefore, served the interests of the most powerful sectors of the economy – goldmining capital and white farmers. In quite different ways, it also favoured, not necessarily equally and not necessarily without contradictory effects, the white fractions of the working class and petite-bourgeoisie – for example, by reducing competion from black workers for jobs and from black traders in the retail trade. For other white classes, for example, manufacturing industrialists, white domination also had both positive and negative effects – positive in the sense that the existence of the racial order was both a condition of its growth through the maintenance of a supply of cheap labour and, yet, at the same time, retarded its expansion by limiting the development of the home market for its products by virtue of the very cheapness of that labour and the dependency of migrant workers, for their reproduction, on the production of a portion of their means of survival on their land within the African Reserves.

This suggests that white domination has never existed as a complete, integrated and internally harmonious system, discordant only at the point of its 'external' imposition on the black people of South Africa. Indeed, the very terms upon which South Africa was constituted as an independent state in 1910 were the subject of intense conflicts within the white population. Despite this, conventionally, white politics was seen to be organised more or less exclusively along the ethnic divide between the Afrikaans and English speaking groups, each group being conceived of as relatively homogeneous and as sharing common interests. Although such an approach obscures the diverse and conflicting interests within the two communities, [2] nevertheless it is undoubtedly the case that, until recently, each of these white communities was largely united around different views of the specific terms upon which white domination should be exercised. These differences notwithstanding, these communities shared a common determination that the black population was to remain the object of and external to the political domain controlled by whites and also subordinated in the economic sphere.

What is evident in the contemporary period, is the weakening of these unities – sharp divisions have appeared within each of the white ethnic groups and the white community no longer presents a completely monolithic united front on the question of white domination. This is expressed, firstly, in the fact that some elements have begun to depart from the former, virtually universal adherence, to an ideology which constitutes blacks as the object of administration rather than the subjects of politics; secondly, in the erosion of the ideology of 'Die Volk' and the appearance of deep fissures among the Afrikaner people which are expressed in conflicting ideologies and organised in different political parties.

It remains the case that the interests of the politically and electorally dominant white groups continue to rest on, and to be defined in terms of, white domination. Even where this is not so, as in the instance of corporate capital which will be discussed below, fear that too radical and too rapid a transformation will result in the demise, not only of apartheid but also of the free enterprise system, results in opposition to apartheid being tempered by an uneasy adherence to the project of white domination.

Nevertheless, the divisions which have become manifest are of considerable importance because they raise the question of the extent to which the white bloc might become politically disorganised as a result of splits within it and 'defections' from it.

What is the basis of these emerging conflicts and how are they to be explained? It is, of course, difficult to separate out the political effects of processes which are occuring simultaneously in the society. It seems clear, for example, that changes in alignments within the white community are due as much to the intense and continuous political struggles of the mass movements against the apartheid system as they are to developments within the economy. We are obliged, however, to analyse these processes separately and I will begin with some elaboration of the economic changes to which I adverted earlier – changes in the class structure at the level of the economic sphere which contribute to the re-definition of class interests.

The repression of the 1960s established a level of stability which, viewed against the turmoil of the 1950s and the events at the time of Sharpeville, proved extremely attractive to foreign capital investors. Direct foreign investment rose between 1960 and 1970 from R1819 million to R3943 million. In addition, national capital (owned within the English and Afrikaner communities) also took advantage of the newly-created opportunities to increase their levels of investment. There are four features of the vast economic growth which ensued which are relevant to class realignments in the present conjuncture.

First, the expansion in both industry and agriculture and, indeed, mining took place on the basis of capital intensification and this was accompanied by a rapid and quite exceptional concentration of capital. [3] Whatever criterion is used – volume of output, capital assets or whatever – all the evidence points to the same conclusion: that there is an unprecedented concentration of economic power in South Africa in the hands of some seven conglomerates which include Anglo-American, Anglo-Vaal, and Barlow Rand. The investment in technology and the resulting mechanisation of production in industry, agriculture, and to a lesser extent, in mining where, nonetheless, a major rationalisation of the labour process occurred, had important effects on the labour requirements of these three sectors of the economy. For one thing, the demand for cheap black labour began to give way to demands for stable, better trained and more productive labour. This is not to suggest that the mechanisation process led to a vast expansion of skilled manual jobs; to some extent there was an increase in the demand for skilled labour, but the major development was the fragmentation of skilled occupations with an emphasis on semi-skilled work at the expense of unskilled.

The demands of the productive economy, for such a labour force, could no longer be met from the available pool of white labour for a number of reasons. Among these were the fact that the expansion of the industrial economy was accompanied, in typical fashion, by a rapid and massive growth in technological and managerial occupations in that sector and financial, managerial and administrative occupations in the expanded tertiary sector. These new occupations made possible a continuous, although uneven, process of upward mobility for many (although by no means all) white employees, thereby creating shortages of labour at other levels of the occupational structure. Secondly, this was aggravated, at a later date, by the conscription of whites into the army. Conscription involves an initial two year period of full-time service and participation in follow-up camps for up to 3 months each for whites between the ages of eighteen and sixty years.

Although black labour began to be recruited into a range of occupations, particularly in the tertiary sector, previously restricted to whites, employers were prevented from extending this process into all occupations, more especially, in mining and the industrial sector. The Job Reservation clause of the Industrial Conciliation Act precluded this (although it was to a certain extent evaded) in a range of occupations as did the resistance of those sections of the white working class who remained in manual occupations. White workers' control over entry into the occupational structure became once more, as it had done frequently in the past, a focus of conflict between capital and black labour on the one side and capital and white labour on the other. But, the conditions in which this conflict took place in the past were unconducive to any serious or permanent erosion of the racialisation of the occupational structure. These conditions were, more especially, the existence of a weak and relatively unorganised black working class faced by a politically powerful white working class supported by the state. These conditions have altered and, although skill monopolies still exist, the protection and sustenance previously accorded by the regime to the Afrikaner classes bound together in the 'Volk' has tended to become far more equivocal than in the past vis à vis the working class. It is clear that in a number of industries, the removal of job reservation apart, the regime has refused to give undiluted support to white workers who have protested against the 'intrusion' of black workers into white preserves.

Secondly, the economic expansion which followed Sharpeville, entailed a restructuring of class relations within the Afrikaner community and this is of particular pertinence to the break up of the ideological and organisational formation of the Afrikaner 'Volk'. As O'Meara (1983) has shown, the development of an Afrikaner capitalist class was, in the 1930s, based on 'communal capital' raised through the various community organisations of the Afrikaans-speaking population and invested in banking and insurance. But, this development was slow and constrained since it came up against the economic power of foreign capital and of an indigenous capitalist class which was, in the main, drawn from the English-speaking community. The election of the National Party to power in 1948 gave Afrikaner capitalists and the aspiring petite bourgeoisie access, via the political, to the means of accelerating their expansion. The process was still relatively slow but, nevertheless, by the end of the 1970s a powerful Afrikaner fraction of corporate capital had developed with interlocking links in a range of economic sectors with other fractions of capital. This occurred both through the successful operation of Afrikaner-held companies and the centralisation of Afrikaner and English capital in the same corporations. Afrikaner large-scale capital, no less than other similarly placed capital has begun to question the functionality of white domination for capitalism.

The same considerations do not, however, apply to that sector of capital which is relatively small-scale and labour intensive for, in this case, the competitive capacity of the enterprises continues to depend on the availability of a supply of cheap black labour. A crucial condition of this is a docile and controllable black labour force. This, in turn, depends on the existence of an unorganised black working class and the reproduction of the structures of white domination.

In the earlier period of the National Party's regime, the aspirant Afrikaner petite bourgeoisie were given strong support by the state – financial support, licences and other assistance. At the same time a major step was taken to undermine competition from Indian traders through the introduction of the Group Areas Act which was used to force these traders out of trading sites in areas declared to be for occupation by whites. African traders at this stage were already operating under regulations which were extremely restrictive. These were, in fact, made more stringent thereby ensuring that this small and struggling sector of business would be unable to compete against state supported Afrikaner traders and small-scale businessmen.

By the mid-1980s, the situation of African small business in the urban areas had undergone a quite emphatic change in part due to the enormous growth of the African consumer market which was a concomitant of the economic expansion of the 1960s and 1970s, and in part due to some encouragement offered by the regime which began to remove restrictions on access to capital and some of the legal obstacles which had previously blocked their growth. The further political implications of this will be discussed later; here it is necessary to note only this (partial) shift of the regime towards encouraging, to some extent, the expansion of the black petite-bourgeoisie. What makes this particularly pointed is the fact that the intrusion of agri-business into agriculture and the concentration of agricultural holdings (which had the support of, and was deliberately fostered by, the Department of Agriculture) has had the effect of driving small scale Afrikaner farmers off the land into the urban areas where the relatively low level of state assistance to enable them to resettle has been a cause for complaint.

Fourthly, the expansion of the 1960s saw an unprecedented growth in the tertiary and manufacturing sectors which, by far, outstrip mining and agriculture in terms of product and employment. The development in manufacturing is indicated by the following statistics:

Table 1    *Employment By Sectors*

| Year | Agriculture | Mining | Manufacturing |
|------|-------------|--------|---------------|
| 1951 | 1,508,642 | 510,091 | 502,100 |
| 1960 | 1,687,486 | 614,582 | 643,520 |
| 1970 | 2,482,452 | 680,384 | 1,026,082 |
| 1980 | 1,299,840 | 820,300 | 1,456,760 |

Source: Central Statistical Services, *South African Statistics*, 1982.

| Table 2 | Percentage Sectoral Contribution to Gross Domestic Product | | |
|---------|-------------|---------|---------------|
| Year | Agriculture | Mining | Manufacturing |
| 1950 | 14.5 | 15.1 | 16.5 |
| 1960 | 11.9 | 17.8 | 19.1 |
| 1970 | 8.3 | 18.3 | 21.2 |
| 1980 | 8.5 | 11.5 | 25.6 |

Source: Central Statistical Services, *South African Statistics*, 1982.

The manufacturing sector produces a certain amount of export commodities, but its major outlet was and is the home market. This market was deepened as a result of white prosperity during the economic boom of the 1960 and early 1970s, but its most significant expansion has come about as a result of the considerable increase in the black labour force. The importance of black consumers has been starkly revealed by the recent boycott of white-owned shops in different parts of the country. The black labour force has expanded from approximately 500,000 in 1960 to over 1,500,000 in the manufacturing industry and, from 1,100,000 to just under 2,000,000 over the same period, in the tertiary sector. Given the limited availablity of export markets, the growth of manufacturing depends heavily on the intensification and extensification of the home market which the labour force provides. Clearly, the reproduction of cheap black labour and the extension and intensification of the home market stand in contradiction to one another. For large-scale capital the position seems clear; but for capital dependent on cheap labour the situation is far more equivocal.

To sum up, our analysis shows that within the white community the relationship between political and economic interests has become extremely complex and varied and this is reflected in the differences, between specific groups, concerning their adherence to or abandonment of, to whatever extent, the racial ordering of the society. This has important implications for the political sphere, but before these are examined it is first necessary to analyse the class situation within the black population, concentrating on the African majority, since this provides an account of the constituencies towards whom reformist policies are directed.

*Class Structure Within the African Community*
In part the transformations in class structure of the African population

was discussed in the previous sub-section and was also referred to in Chapters 2 and 4. It is only necessary now to summarise what has already been said and to supplement this in two respects.

It has been shown that the African industrial working class and the African work force in the tertiary sector have increased massively over the past 25 years. In addition, an urban black petite-bourgeosie whose growth has depended on the development of a black consumer market of urban wage earners, has been identified with its organisation in the National African Chamber of Commerce. Some elements of this class have begun to constitute, via commercial undertakings and banking, a small class of African merchant and financial capitalists.

In the bantustans, the bulk of the population are impoverished, often landless, agricultural producers, pastoralists, migrant workers and unemployed, but a process of class formation has been taking place. A 'bureaucratic' bourgeoisie, [4] an expanded petite bourgeoisie and, indeed, also a class of agricultural capitalists has emerged in these areas. The existence and fate of these classes is tied to an essential component of the apartheid structure − it is precisely positions in the bureaucratic and legislative bodies of the bantustans that gives access to land, finance, trading licences and other resources which makes possible the expanded reproduction of this class. Here ethnicity has become a crucial factor in the formation of certain classes and the pursuit of the interests of those classes has became bound up with ethnic identities and positions. The prime, but not the only example, is the Zulu-based organisation, Inkatha.

THE STRUCTURES OF REFORM

The strategic problem facing the regime from the mid-1970s was extremely complex. The priority was, and remains, the containment of the mass democratic opposition by coercive means precisely because the protection of white interests precludes a process of state-led radical reform. At the same time, the government has been unable to resist completely pressures for reforms from those sections of the white population discussed above, supported by a tendency within the regime itself. Furthermore, these reforms entail measures which are both aimed at the cooptation of the black petite-bourgeoisie and bourgeoisie and at limiting their political effects by 'economising' the demands which become possible by virtue of the reforms.

The regime has established and revised institutional structures in two different areas which are particularly pertinent to the process of political reform − industrial relations and black representation. It is not possible to trace through the changes in these areas over the past ten years and my intention is merely to lay the basis for a discussion of the political effects of the reform measures.

*The Institutional Structure of Industrial Relations.*
The Industrial Conciliation Amendment Act 94 of 1979 amended the 1926 Industrial Conciliation Act. The 1926 legislation, by specifically excluding 'pass bearing' persons from the definition of 'employee' for the purposes of the Act, made it impossible for Africans to organise legally recognised trade unions. The deletion of this exclusion, together with other provisions of the 1979 amending act, resulted in black workers, under restrictive conditions, acquiring the right to establish trade unions. On registration, unions would be brought into the industrial conciliation procedures. The Act also established an Industrial Court to hear disputes arising out of laws administered by the Department of Labour as well as disputes between employers and workers.

The provisions of the Act thus established the apparatuses of the state aimed at the institutionalisation of industrial conflict and, as a concomitant of this, the isolation of the black trade union movement from broader political movements and its canalisation into strictly trade union activities concerned with working conditions and wages.

*Black Political Representation*
The restructuring of institutions of black representation and the apparatuses of control of 'black affairs' has been at the heart of the regime's strategy. This restructuring process has occurred both within and also outside of the bantustans.

Prior to 1973, the bantustan policy was, of course, well under way but the structures of bantustan administration, including the granting of 'independence' in some cases were further developed. The complex of political and economic structures established in the bantustans has erected a political sphere characterised, on the one hand, by the existence of subordinate state apparatuses and, on the other hand, by the virtual absence of a terrain of politics outside of those structures – apart from emasculated political parties and, increasingly to-day, the organisation of opposition to the bantustan system as a whole.[5]

The consequence is that a political sub-system has been instituted in which the subordinate bantustan states act as agents for the regime (although not always without a certain degree of resistance) in exercising control over the 'internal' polity and economy in the bantustans and, thereby, establish the conditions for the development of a black 'bureaucratic' bourgeoisie.

This has been accomplished by the creation of an institutional order which has shifted certain roles, previously performed by the central state, to the bantustan authorities including: military forces trained and equipped by the South African regime; the administration of education; local magistrate courts and an administrative structure both of which were previously under the control of the Bantu Affairs Department; economic planning by the legislative assemblies, although the development corporations funded by the South African state in fact determine development strategies; legislative assemblies elected by the people living in the bantustans although the balance of power is held by appointed officials and chiefs who are ex officio members of the assembly.

Outside of the bantustans, the regime has established political structures at local, regional and national level.

Under the Community Councils Act 1977, provision was made for the election of community councils in African townships outside the bantustans. These councils were to have limited powers over local affairs including housing. Their sources of income were rents and service charges but the central government made no financial contribution. By 1982, 230 councils had been elected by a minute percentage of eligible voters.

The failure of these councils as instruments of local government led to the passing of the Black Local Authorities Act of 1982. This act provided for the election of town and village councils with more powers than the community councils. These included: control of street trading, the provision and maintenance of services such as rubbish removal and sewage disposal, electricity, water and roads. The town and village councils remained dependent on rents and service charges for their income. The first elections, with an even lower poll than for the community councils, took place in 1983.

In 1984, the government announced that the town and village councils were to be integrated into the regional government system established in 1983. Two bodies in that system are of particular relevance. Firstly, the Council for Co-ordination of Local Government Affairs which originally consisted only of Whites, Coloureds and Indians largely appointed by the Minister of Constitutional Development. These were government officials, representatives of local and provincial government and representatives of the White, Indian and Coloured Councils of Ministers which will be referred to below. In 1984 representatives of black local authorities were added. The function of this body is to promote change in local and regional government.

Secondly, there are the Regional Services Councils which exercise control over and co-ordinate local councils. These Councils consist of government officials and representatives of African, White, Indian and Coloured local councils. While the local councils have jurisdiction over 'own affairs', that is the exercise of local government over the affairs of their own, segregated, communities and areas, the Regional Service Councils are concerned with common matters, that is 'general affairs'.

At the national level, the major innovation was the establishment of the tri-cameral Parliament which came into existence in 1984. The effect of the legislation was to add, alongside the all-white Parliament (House of Assembly), two other houses, one for the representation of the Indian population (House of Delegates) and one for the representation of the Coloured population (House of Representatives). The office of Prime Minister was abolished and replaced by that of the State President who, in terms of the Act, is elected by a college of 50 White, 25 Coloured and 13 Indian members of the tri-cameral Parliament. The State President has the right to dissolve any of the houses that passes a motion of no confidence in the Cabinet which is appointed by him. He has the power to decide what matters are 'own affairs' for the White, Indian and Coloured houses and what are 'general affairs'. 'Own affairs' are to be legislated on by the individual houses, while 'general affairs' are the concern of the Cabinet and legislation must be passed by a majority in each of the three houses. If not, the President's Council or the State President decides on the legislation on the advice of the Council. That Council consists of 5 representatives from the House of Delegates, 10 from the House of Representatives, 20 from the House of Assembly and 25 members nominated by the State President. Executive responsibility of 'own affairs' lies with the Ministers' Councils of each house which are appointed by the State President.

The constitution excludes the African majority except in two respects. One clause provides that 'The control and administration of Black affairs shall rest with the State President' and the other makes 'Black Affairs' the common concern of the tri-cameral Parliament; that is they are defined as part of 'general affairs' and are decided upon in the way set out above by parliamentary structures which exclude Africans.

THE POLITICAL STRUGGLE: POLICIES AND STRATEGIES

I now want to turn to a discussion of the differing policies, strategies and balance of power of the contending forces in the present period as these were conditioned by the structure of the state, the political terrain and the class formation.

It is, of course significant, that the Botha government presents itself as the regime of reform protected by the coercive apparatuses of the state by contrast with previous governments which stressed only their repressive role in maintaining control over the black population. The significance lies in the fact that this shift and its expression in reformist ideologies and the claims to reformist policies has been brought about, in the structural conditions analysed earlier, primarily by the mass democratic opposition whose struggle has put in question, for the first time in South African history, the entire system of white domination and by pressures from within the white community.

From the standpoint of the regime and the reformist sections of the white population, the reformist strategy may be primarily understood as a collection of measures which are aimed at allowing political activity but limiting the objectives which may be pursued and at privileging, to some extent, selected classes or categories of black subjects with the intention of either creating divisions among the black masses, by creating a 'Third Force', or co-optating sections of the population into working with the regime or both. It is in this respect that the 'reform' of the state structures outlined earlier in this chapter are relevant.

The introduction of new apparatuses of the state or the reformation of existing ones to enable reformist policies to be pursued for these purposes does not, of course, guarantee that, in practice, they will be achieved and that political stabilisation will result. It does not follow from the fact that a regime establishes specific state apparatuses that such apparatuses, therefore, will act at its behest or that of a particular class. The state apparatuses are not, that is to say, the simple, unequivocal instruments of a regime (or a class) although in the struggle to give effect to its policies, [6] it is forced to create instruments of state and to strive to obtain and retain control of them.

In the analysis which follows it will first be argued that the regime's attempt to utilise the institutional structure it established to undercut the centre position occupied by the ANC, UDF and COSATU failed and that, secondly, indeed, these structures created the political space which allowed the mass democratic organisations to considerably strengthen their position.

*A Third Force? Reform and Divisions Within the Black Opposition Class, Ethnicity and the Bantustans:* It is clear from the brief discussion above that the regime's policies have facilitated some improvement in the economic position of the black petite-bourgeosie both in the bantustans and in the urban areas. The effect of the bantustan policy has been to form a petite-bourgeoisie and a bureaucratic bourgeoisie whose politics have become centred on the functioning of their state apparatuses. This effect, moreover, is intensified by the fact that the conduct of bantustan politics takes place, given the almost complete absence of a political terrain, beyond the legislative assemblies and the administrative apparatuses of the bantustan sub-states. The politics of the bantustans as conducted through these organs has, both internally and in relation to the apartheid state, taken on an ethnic and 'free market' orientation.

The incorporation of ethnicity into this area of politics operates to divide it from the national liberation movement which rejects the entire bantustan policy and ethnic politics.

The most significant expression of ethnic politics is Inkatha, not only because of its size and degree of organisation but also because it functions within Kwazulu and also intervenes directly, in opposition to the ANC and the UDF and its affiliates, in the political contestations outside of Kwazulu in 'white' South Africa.

Inkatha was established in 1922 but was revived in 1975, adopting the ANC banner and uniform. The stated aim of the organisation was to struggle for the abolition of apartheid through non-violent means using the bantustan structures. It claims a membership of over one million in a thousand branches of which all but 36 are in Natal and Kwazulu. Jobs in Kwazulu and as for migrants elsewhere, promotion, housing and so on are conditional upon Inkatha membership.

Originally, Inkatha's overt opposition to the ANC appeared to be based primarily on a question of strategy – Inkatha's rejection of the armed struggle. There were, however, also policy differences – for example, on the very issue of participation in the bantustan structures – and, furthermore, underlying processes were at work which greatly deepened the divergence between these organisations and between Inkatha and all the organisations of the mass democratic movement. By the early 1980s, Inkatha had become active in violently breaking up meetings of the UDF and its affiliates and assaulting their activists. [7]

The differences between Inkatha and the national liberation movement cannot be reduced merely to doctrinal and strategic disputes between two organisations which are otherwise linked by a common objective, even though Chief Buthelezi (Chief Minister of Kwazulu) fiercely rejects apartheid and 'independence' for Kwazulu. The fact of the matter is that by working within the bantustan structures established by the state, Buthelezi has become enmeshed in its logic and the implications of this, referred to above, for the ethnicisation of politics and for the encouragement of petit bourgeois and small capitalist class interests.

Of course, this is not to argue that the bantustan structures constitute an iron cage which guarantees only one outcome under all conditions, but it certainly functions to limit severely the conditions which might contribute to the possibilities of breaking the mould. This is exemplified by Inkatha which, though a mass organisation, has been fused into the Kwazulu state structures and operates as an instrument of that state.

The divisions between Inkatha–Kwazulu and the democratic movement have been still further entrenched in two different directions. Firstly, the establishment by Inkatha, in opposition to COSATU, of the United Workers Union of South Africa, with a claimed membership of some 60,000 workers.

Secondly, the Kwazulu government and the Natal provincial council have held a series of meetings known as the Kwazulu-Natal Ndaba which resulted in the adoption of a non-racial Bill of Rights intended to apply to the region of Natal and Kwazulu. Although proposals are apparently being formulated which deal with some redistribution of wealth in the region, the Bill of Rights itself makes no reference at all to economic rights and simply leaves intact the gross, racially structured inequalities in property and wealth which are the product pre-eminently of the system of white domination and, to a lesser extent, of the bantustan system itself. Politically, however, the essential point is that the Kwazulu-Natal initiative has to be understood as part of a federal solution to the contemporary crisis. What is common to the various federal schemes that have been proposed as a basis for a negotiated settlement is that they entail no change in the structure or control of state power at the centre where white domination would remain intact.

Inkatha, then, presents itself, in opposition to the national liberation movement organised around the ANC and the United Democratic Front and the independent trade union movement, as the 'moderate' voice of national liberation in opposition to apartheid while, at the same time, operating the key institutions of apartheid and intervening violently against other black organisations. While it is difficult to estimate the extent of support among the Zulu people for Inkatha (partly because of the patronage and strong arm techniques utilised by it), nevertheless, the existence and activities of the organisation, especially given its linkage with the bantustan sub-state, constitute an oppositional force, within the African community, to the national liberation movement. While its significance in this respect and its part in generating a divisive ethnic based politics should not be ignored, the fact remains that precisely because of its ethnic basis the organisation's influence is confined to an uncertain section of the Zulu people. In this sense, it remains marginal to the struggles of the mass democratic organisations which have not only mobilised people without regard to race or ethnicity, but whose combined power has occupied the centre stage of the struggle against apartheid.

*The Black Urban Petite Bourgeoisie:* If the institutional structure of the bantustans externalises and ethnicises petit and bureaucratic bourgeois politics, the situation in the urban areas is quite different. There, encouraged by state policies the emphasis has been on economic structures and advancement. Although the structures of local and regional government discussed earlier have been operated by individuals drawn from the urban black petite bourgeoisie, they have neither been ethnically based nor played an equivalent role in class formation as the bantustan structures.

The possibility of 'economising' the demands of urban African businessmen, by detaching their economic position from government regulation, was taken up in the writings of influential academics at the time when the regime established 'reformist' commissions (e.g. Wiehahn, Riekert) in the late 1970s. What was emphasised was the need to establish a free market economy by removing state controls on housing, the urban labour market and so on. The intervention of the state in these areas, it was argued, turned all demands over these resources into political confrontations. If access to these resources were 'purely economic', market forces would determine distribution, and the issues would thereby be de-politicised. The same argument was echoed in a number of places within the state departments and in the Riekert Commission proposals.

In fact, the opposition to apartheid of, at least, the organised sections of the African petite bourgeoisie largely took the form of demands for economic reforms, a virtual silence being maintained on the question of political rights and power. Indeed, the National African Chamber of Commerce (NAFCOC) invoked apartheid policies to preserve monopolies over trade in the African townships when white-controlled merchant capital sought the right to open hypermarkets in these lucrative trading areas. Again, during the 1976 Soweto crisis NAFCOC took a very hostile public stance against the students. [8]

The functioning of the urban councils established by the state has depended very much on the participation of individuals drawn from this class who have been prepared to offer themselves as candidates in elections. But it is to be noted that the polls in these elections have been minute and despite the replacement of the community councils by town and village councils with greater powers, the percentage of eligible voters declined. It is clear that there is no mass following for those sections of the petit bourgeoisie who are prepared to collaborate with the regime.

Furthermore, there is very little popular support for these institutions of local government. More exactly, there has been virtual outright rejection of these bodies as shown by the extensive rent and service charges boycotts which have severely impaired the capacity of these organs of local government to operate effectively. Numerous urban townships. People prepared to work the urban councils established by the state in the townships has been drawn. That is, politics for this group is legitimate when it conforms to state policy.

More recently, urban black business has become somewhat emboldened by the strength of the mass movement and has begun to pursue its own limited demands in a more forthright manner. [9] Moreover, in 1986, the National African Chamber of Conference appeared, tentatively, to be moving closer to the ANC and the liberation movement. Not only has it called for the participation of banned leaders and organisations in negotiations with the regime, but also it issued a joint communique after a meeting with the ANC which stated: 'The urgent task facing all our people is to find a solution to the crisis which has engulfed our country'. However, it has also sent a delegation to the government to ask for government funding to restart business destroyed in the 'unrest'.

Overall, organised African business in the urban areas has pursued its own economic interests. Its collective role in wider politics has been muted and ambiguous as the above examples of its activities demonstrates. Individually, members of this class have been actively engaged in state-established local government structures and in business enterprises with white capital. In summary, neither the policy of the organisations of this class nor the activities of individuals has secured popular support.

*The Black Trade Unions:* In relation to the working class, there is evidence that the government attempted to drive a rift between urban and migrant workers and, indeed, the act granting trade union rights originally excluded the latter. Be that as it may, a central thrust of the regime's strategy (frequently abetted by employers) has been to try to control the unions and, in particular, to ensure that they remain separated from the national liberation struggle and confine their demands and activities to wages and conditions of work. In other words the strategy was to make the unions restrict themselves to economic demands. To this end a variety of tactics have been employed. Thus, a condition of legal recognition and registration of the unions is that they must confine themselves strictly to trade union matters; again, politically-oriented trade union officials and activists have been detained without trial, subjected to torture, charged with treason and so on; finally, unions which have taken up broad political issues and aligned themselves with community organisations and the political movements have been met with repressive action.

In fact, this strategy of the regime directly affected the independent trade union movement since, in the early 1980s, a split occurred over the two related issues of whether unions should register under the Act and whether or not the unions should involve themselves directly in the national liberation struggle or confine themselves to shop floor issues. Ultimately, the state removed the one issue by making registered and unregistered unions subject to the industrial relations legislation, thereby removing the objections to registration.

The second issue was resolved in the unity conference which resulted in the formation of COSATU in December 1985 and the dissolution into it of the Federation of South African Trade Unions, which had been, at least at leadership level, the major protagonist of the restricted role for trade unions. Although the black trade union movement is still not fully united, and divisions between COSATU on the one side and CUSA and AZACTU still exist, albeit on a diminishing scale, nevertheless the formation of COSATU in December 1985 united a large number of unions in a federation on the basis of a commitment to the broad aims of the national liberation movement. The question for COSATU is not whether it should involve itself in political struggles, but rather, how it should do this. The participation of the unions in the 1986 May Day stay-at-home and the demands (coupled with the threat of strikes) for an ending of the state of emergency declared in June 1986 are examples. The tendency for the unions to be drawn beyond the boundaries of strictly trade union issues is strong and continuous – the insistence of the 100,000 strong National Union of Mineworkers on linking political and trade union issues is only one instance. The state has, therefore, failed to isolate the independent trade union movement from the liberation struggle.

*The Tri-Cameral Parliament:* Finally, it is necessary to touch on the participation of Indian and Coloured organisations in the tri-cameral Parliament. The decision of the Coloured Labour Party (CLP) to take part in the elections to the tri-cameral Parliament and to work the new constitution split the party. A number of prominent members resigned, arguing that it was not possible to oppose apartheid from within these state apparatuses. Rather, the effect would be to collaborate in mechanisms which reinforce apartheid under the guise of a reformist rhetoric. In practice, the Indian and CLP representatives have played an extremely ambiguous role in the Parliament.

On the one hand, they have announced that they will open the schools under their jurisdiction to all 'racial' groups; and have threatened to take action against the largely white group which controls the University of Durban, Westville because of evidence of racist practices by this group; they refused to pass the Public Safety Amendment Bill which would have enabled the regime to declare certain areas to be 'unrest areas' and to follow this by giving the police and the South African Defence Force extremely wide powers. On the other hand, the Indian and Coloured parliamentary parties have attempted to force boycotting pupils back to school; they have confirmed the dismissal of activist teachers and made barely any protest against the extensive detentions, emergency powers and violence of the state.

However, the crucial point here is that these organisations have very little popular support for their involvement in the institutional structure of the tri-cameral Parliament. This was shown not only in the extremely small vote at the elections but, more particularly, by the pre-occupation of the people with political actions against the regime which are totally unconnected with the parliamentary system.

The regime has thus substantially failed in its policy to divide the liberation movement or to establish a plausible 'third force' through these strategies.

*Reforms and the Consolidation of the Mass Democratic Movement*
The failure of reforms to dampen the radical thrust of the opposition by developing a third force or to produce political stabilisation is attributed, by both the national liberation movement and liberal reformers, to the fact that they are simply cosmetic and do not go far enough. This is undoubtedly correct, but in simply writing off the reforms as cosmetic, their political significance tends to be overlooked.

For it is clear that some important changes have been introduced – the legalisation of the black trade unions is perhaps the most important case in point. Be that as it may, the development of a reformist policy has, however cosmetic, called forth apparatuses which are new and different to those previously in existence, and which are intended to function to give effect to the reforms. Whether they do so or do not, as was argued in Chapter 1, the crucial point is that the establishment of these apparatuses opens, under the protection of the reforms, new fields of struggle. It is important, therefore, to emphasise the manner in which the restructuring of the state permits consequences other than those intended by the regime.

The reformist measures, in particular the provisions for urban black political representation, the tri-cameral Parliament and the recognition of black trade unions (together with the expansion of schools and universities which was discussed above) created a political space within which the opposition organisations were able to deepen their links in the communities and consolidate themselves. The point is that these legal institutions, in various ways (election campaigns in the case of urban representation and the tri-cameral Parliament and trade union organisation under the industrial legislation) provided legitimate arenas, in which the intervention of the coercive apparatuses of the state was relatively limited. In allowing elections, whether for the urban councils or the tri-cameral Parliament, the regime, at the same time, legitimated campaigns around those elections even where the campaigns were directed towards a boycott of them. Likewise, once trade unions were recognised it proved extremely difficult for the state to enforce the 'no politics' provisions of the legislation. These actions enabled, for example, the UDF organisations to consolidate their position in the townships.

In considering the utilisation of legal political space, it is also of great importance to recognise the changed role of the judiciary in the period after 1976.

The resort to law and the idea of a judicary independent of other state structures, as I have already suggested, have been tenacious features of the South African state. Nonetheless, it is incontrovertible that both through the provisions of the law, which derogated from the powers of the courts, through direct and indirect political pressures on judicial officers and the appointment of judges favourable to the regime, the autonomy of the judiciary was considerably reduced during the 1960s and beyond. What is of considerable interest is the fact that the rise of the mass movement, after 1973, provided the conditions for the judicial space to broaden. Judges became bolder and began to use to the full the narrow legal space and, indeed, to put some pressure on its existing limits. In recent years, the judges have begun to give judgments which challenge, in certain respects, the power of the executive and the security forces over individual rights.

This was reflected in the Supreme Court's reversal, in 1979 and 1983, of earlier judgments in which the rights of Africans under the Urban Areas Act were restrictively interpreted in favour of the state.

Furthermore, there have been a number of judgments which directly affect rights as these have been curtailed, inter alia, by emergency regulations: for example, the setting aside of banning orders imposed without the affected person being given a hearing; emergency regulations have been strictly construed to give trade unions the right to hold indoor meetings despite a general ban on meetings; detainees have gained the right of access to lawyers and newspaper curbs have been declared too wide and therefore beyond the powers of the police.

This is not to suggest that these judicial challenges to the executive are sufficent, on their own, to establish an unassailable independence from the executive. Firstly, not all judges, by any means, exercise their judicial powers in this way and, indeed, many continue in the old way. Secondly, the state has not hesitated to introduce new laws or regulations to render decisions against it nugatory. Nonetheless, it is important to note that the re-emergence of the play of contradictory relations between judiciary and the executive has also been a condition of the deepening of the terrain of extra-parliamentary mass politics.

## 'Render South Africa Ungovernable'

It was the spread, strengthening and unification of these organisations which provided the conditions in which the campaign to 'render South Africa ungovernable' took root. The manifestations of this campaign were widespread and varied – boycott of schools, elections and shops, refusal to pay rents and service charges, continuous demonstrations, strikes and stay-at-homes, violent community confrontations with the police and army and armed actions by Umkhonto

We Sizwe against state forces and installations. The outcome of these actions was the collapse, in many areas, of the local apartheid structures. The regime responded in July 1985 by imposing a state of emergency which was lifted in March 1986 in anticipation of the visit by the Eminent Persons Group.

The slogan 'make South Africa ungovernable' began to be displaced by the call for 'people's power' and during the emergency rudimentary organs of people's power, in particular street committees, were established in black townships. As the President of the Border Region of the UDF put it:

> Within the ensuing vacuum we have seen the remarkable . . . emergence countrywide of rudimentary organs of people's power. In particular, democratic street committees, elected house by house, street by street, have developed . . . in a large number of townships and villages. Suddenly, many of the most severe problems that had plagued our ghettoes have been resolved, like weekend violence, gangsterism, rape. A strange paradox this, as the authorities have collapsed, as black policemen have packed up and fled from the townships, so, strange, to say, we have seen a dramatic drop in the level of violent crime.
>
> This has been the experience countrywide. It is limited to the development of basic democratic control over the streets by the people themselves. These have become our own liberated zones, not in the remote countryside but in the backyard of an industrial society.

In addition a number of alternative functional organisations appeared on the scene. The latter include alternative, non-racial bodies such as the National Medical and Dental Association, Health Workers' Association, the Organisation for Appropriate Social Science in South Africa, the Legal Resources Centre, various adult education organisations, alternative news agencies and so on.

In short, the depth of resistance to, and the extent of popular participation in politics directed against the state and its apparatuses of control, was manifested in the organic links established between the community and political organisations and the people in the urban communities. Moreover, the communities themselves, in many parts of the country, became transformed into political bodies of opposition – with the people organised as a political force. It is these developments which reveal the extent of the failure of the regime's reformist strategy to divide and displace the major thrust of the opposition and of the failure of the 1985–1986 emergency to curb its development.

*An Unstable Balance of Power*
In this period, although the regime did take emergency powers and deployed military and police forces, it was constrained from attempting to take even more extreme coercive measures by external pressures on it from the USA, Britain and West Germany, the Commonwealth and internal pressures from corporate capital and more liberal forces within its own ranks. The coercion it exercised was not sufficient to destroy or curb the mass movement and in consequence the mass movement was given the time to sink its roots deeper into the community.

If the regime was unable to destroy the terrain of extra-parliamentary mass politics in the 1980s as it had done with such rapidity in the 1960s, nor was the mass democratic movement yet in a position to dislodge the regime. In short, there existed an unstable equilibrium in which the white bloc, while holding state power and having at its disposal the armed and security forces, was unable to suppress the mass opposition which, in turn, did not have the immediate capacity to overthrow the regime and the system.

In this situation a space was opened up for initiatives for a reformist solution to the country's crisis on the basis of a 'negotiated settlement'.

*A Negotiated Settlement?*
The major initiatives for a reformist settlement to be based on negotiations between the regime and the ANC and other oppositional forces have come from large scale capital and its major political representative, the Progressive Federal Party. The PFP has also worked closely with the Urban Foundation – an organisation established with funds from large corporations – and with Chief Buthelezi's Inkatha movement which opposes the armed struggle of the ANC and calls for a negotiated settlement.

Strong international pressure has been brought to bear on the regime to negotiate with the ANC. Previously, USA and British policy was structured around the notion of 'constructive engagement' which envisaged, as it were, a dialogue between these states and the South African regime with the purpose of encouraging the latter to bring about reforms for the black people who would be and were absent from the dialogue. With the rise of the popular movement and the obvious impossibility of a 'negotiated settlement' without the participation of the ANC, 'constructive engagement' has come to be seen as an engagement between the regime and the ANC.

The regime's capacity to offer an acceptable basis for a negotiated settlement or, indeed, participate in negotiations is extremely limited. The reason for this is that, even if the rather unlikely assumption is made that its verligte (enlightened) wing is prepared to agree to a

103

non-racial democratic society – one person one vote – the regime itself is subject to extremely severe constraints from its social base. It was pointed out earlier, that the main electoral base of the National Party is among those sections of the white population who see reforms which go beyond those the government is at present offering, to be a threat to their ever-vulnerable positions of privilege, status and profit and hence unacceptable. Moreover, to secure its position against the inroads which extreme right-wing Afrikaner parties are making on its popular support, the National Party tends to adopt repression rather than reform and negotiation as its policy.

The government's antipathy to negotiation was abundantly displayed when it scuttled the attempt by the Commonwealth Eminent Persons Group to set up negotiations between the ANC and the government, by bombing allegedly ANC military targets in Zimbabwe, Zambia and Botswana.

From the side of the national liberation movement there are two different reasons why a negotiated settlement with the regime seems not possible. The first relates to the narrow limits of the possible reforms in relation to the demands of the liberation movement as set out in the Freedom Charter. The second relates to the fact that whatever political reforms the regime concedes in advance to be open for discussion, the possibility of negotiation would be undermined by its continued control of the army and the security forces.

The first obstacle to a negotiated settlement is the nature of the demands around which the national liberation movement is organised. There is no single programme which completely unites the whole of the black mass opposition. The Freedom Charter commands most support although, as was pointed out in Chapter 2, it is not free of some ambiguity and it may not go far enough for some. The National Forum and AZAPO, for example, contend that the Freedom Charter is unacceptable because, inter alia, it does not embody a socialist perspective and for this reason these organisations do not work in a common front with the UDF or the ANC. Despite this, there is no doubt that, whether the Freedom Charter goes far enough or not, its provisions embody claims which are endorsed by the entire black mass opposition to the regime.

What is common to mass democratic opposition is the demand for the dismantling of apartheid and the establishment of a unitary democratic political system based on one person one vote, together with some degree of redistribution of the economic resources as outlined in the Freedom Charter. What is involved, as a minimum, over and above the political demands is: (a) the dismantling of the giant corporations which now exercise decisive power over all sectors of the South African economy, in order to ensure that a non-racial democratic regime can exercise a degree of control over the major economic resources in agriculture, industry, mining and finance; (b) the rapid removal of the extreme inequalities in access to land through its radical redistribution and (c) the massive redistribution of resources in education, welfare, housing, health and so forth in favour of the black people, which even a reformed capitalism would be unable to undertake. It is implicit that the transformation of South African society in this direction depends pre-eminently on the development of structures of 'peoples' power' based on the working class and the full involvement of the democratic trade unions and the mass organisations of the people.

The second circumstance which renders a negotiated settlement highly questionable for the national liberation movement is the extreme imbalance between it and the state in terms of military power.

In South Africa, at present, the core of the opposition to apartheid is in the mass political struggle and trade union struggles, particularly in the urban areas. It seems clear that the presence and actions of the military wing of the ANC, Umkhonto We Sizwe (MK), are an extremely important support for these actions in terms of 'armed propaganda' and as part of the assault on the regime. Yet, MK has not yet been established as a fully-fledged guerilla force comparable, for example, to the Patriotic Front's army in Zimbabwe. The insurrectionary movement remains the major mode of struggle.

In Zimbabwe, the situation was quite different. There, the main instrument of the national liberation struggle was the guerilla army of the Patriotic Front. It was this army which forced the Smith regime to the negotiating table. But what was crucial was the fact that the guerilla army had the means to continue the main struggle during the period of negotiatons and, equally importantly, had the capacity to guarantee, in the aftermath of the settlement, that the gains of the settlement were not snatched back by the former regime. Thus, in Zimbabwe, where the army was locked into the structures of the white regime with little prospect of it disintegrating as, for example, in Iran in 1979, it could only be held in check, after negotiations, by a powerful guerilla army. In South Africa such a guerilla force does not yet exist.

*Breaking the Equilibrium*
While, clearly, conditions may arise in the future which will permit negotiations towards a settlement (although it is extremely difficult to envisage what they might be) under existing circumstances, there is little possibility of such a solution to the political crisis.

The question, then, which is posed for both the regime and the national liberation movement is how the unstable equilibrium may be decisively shifted in one direction or another? That is to say, what will enhance the capacity of the regime to stabilise the situation and

105

introduce and maintain a reformed system of racial domination with the white bloc unequivocally still in power? Or, by contrast, what are the conditions which will accord the oppositional forces the capacity to defeat the regime and set in place a non-racial, democratic state? The situation is extremely volatile and it is not my purpose either to predict the outcome or to attempt to discuss in detail the events occurring at the time of writing. Rather, I want to conclude by identifying, briefly and schematically, the parameters of the unfolding struggle.

The declaration by the regime of a state of emergency in June 1986, three months after the ending of the previous emergency, appears to have signalled the beginning of a new strategy aimed at turning the balance in its favour. The strategy has two main features. Firstly, the utilisation of extraordinary emergency powers to destroy the community and political organisations. This has included exceptionally tight controls on the media so that political actions and the handling of them by the military and the police cannot be reported without state permission; the arrest of over 4000 political activists; the banning of meetings; the harrassment of political workers and street committees; and the continued presence of the military and security forces in the townships.

Furthermore, the regime has intensified its use of physical repression and, in this respect, has taken advantage of the poverty and unemployment of millions of people in the bantustans to build up a force of state-vigilantes to work under the authority of police. The state-vigilante groups have become notorious for their brutality against members of the UDF and its affiliates. The state-vigilantes are thus coupled with the military and police forces in the townships and the strong arm forces of Inkatha, to constitute a formidable coercive weapon designed to emasculate the political opposition.

Despite all these measures, it is manifest that even with the exercise of extreme emergency powers over some ten months, the regime has largely failed to destroy the mass democratic organisations and to restore the political stability of the 1960s. This is not to suggest that the use of emergency powers has not had significant effects on these organisations – it is clear that mass arrests, the banning of meetings and other punitive actions have resulted in the severe impairment of many local organisations and, in some areas, the street committees have ceased functioning. Nonetheless, many organisations have found new, underground and semi-legal ways of operating as have recently formed organisations such as the South African Youth Congress and the South African National Students Congress; numerous street committees continue to work as does the UDF, the NECC and the alternative functional organisations described above; and the black trade unions continue unabated.

How much further can the regime proceed with its attempts to destroy the mass democratic movement?

It seems apparent that notwithstanding the enormous emergency powers that the regime has been able to deploy, its capacity to eliminate the mass democratic movement has, in terms of its present mode of operation, virtually exhausted itself. This has led some commentators and, indeed, some government ministers to suggest that the next step open to the regime is a 'Chilean' solution, that is to say the physical obliteration of thousands of political activists. But is such a path open to the regime? A number of factors suggest that it is not.

The first of these relates to the capacity of the street committees, political, community and trade union organisations to withstand the state's repressive policy. That capacity depends above all on the close meshing of communities and political organisations and this is of particular relevance to the street committees. In this respect South Africa differs from Chile – for in South Africa the destruction of the political organisations would entail not merely the eradication of cadres but the virtual decimation of certain sections of the urban communities. Furthermore, it is extremely likely that such a move would provoke a ferocious armed resistance from all black communities – already the youth in the black townships have made insistent demands to be provided with arms and have, in fact, to some extent armed themselves.

The political capacity of the regime, in any event, to undertake such a venture, is extremely circumscribed. Although it would undoubtedly have the backing of the extreme right wing groupings, it is unlikely to have the undivided support of those whites who vote for the Progressive Federal Party or even of its own electoral constituency which has tended to favour a mildly reformist path. Furthermore, there are increasing indications of the weakening of the cohesion of the regime's social base and of intensifying contradictions within the white bloc. These centrifugal pressures are reflected in the growing and persistent splits to the right of the National Party and, more recently, in the public emergence of both intellectual and political divisions in favour of 'bridge building' and further reforms to the 'left' of the party. Undoubtedly, these centrifugal tendencies act to constrain the regime's room for manoeuvre in the direction of a still more violently repressive policy.

In addition, international opposition to such a policy, both from individual countries – including the major Western powers – and from international organisations cannot be discounted despite the government's apparent disregard.

Over and above these political factors, the government's capacity to eradicate the political opposition is limited by the extraordinary demands on state resources in the contemporary period. The maintenance and reproduction of the structures of white domination entail enormous manpower, financial and material resources – this is one of the reasons for the reformist position of corporate capital.

On the one hand, the bureaucratic and security apparatuses and the coercive measures absorb a huge and increasing proportion of the state's resources; the occupation by the police and army of the townships (particularly during the state of emergency), the state-vigilantes and conscription are major items in this regard. On the other hand, additional economic demands are made on the regime's resources by the costs of the reform programme for blacks, however limited these may be, and by the necessity, at the same time, of maintaining white privileges.

Finally, in this respect, it is necessary to consider South Africa's position in the southern African region. South Africa established dominance over the countries in the region, long before the accession to power of the present regime, through investments, migrant labour, customs agreements and transportation. What is unique about the present situation is that the defence of apartheid against the *internal opposition* requires, at the same time, the political and economic subordination of all the neighbouring states in the Southern African region.

The reason for this is that the direction and development of the internal struggles have been, and continue to be, fundamentally shaped by the political role of the ANC and its armed wing, Umkhonto We Sizwe and one or other or both these organisations have been given support and sustenance in the different neighbouring regional states.

While these organisations exist, white domination remains under threat and no more so than in the present conjuncture. For the regime it is, therefore, necessary to utterly undermine or destroy them. For this purpose, the regime has embarked upon political, economic and military intervention in the regional states and given considerable support, for example, to Unita in Angola and the MNR in Mocambique. The object is to force these countries to curtail or expel the ANC and to refuse rear bases to Umkhonto. To achieve this the government is obliged to commit massive resources.

It seems clear that the regime is extremely widely stretched and it follows that any substantial increase in the costs of maintaining its position of power or any decline in the level of resources available to it, must threaten its capacity to hold the democratic mass movement in check. Clearly, this situation would be affected by a deepening of the economic crisis, by more effective international sanctions, by an increase in the costs of dominating the regional states (which may happen if they obtain additional aid from the developed countries) and by an escalation of the internal conflict, which would occur if a still more violent internal policy were pursued.

If the arguments advanced in this section are correct, it follows that the regime is unable to resolve the crisis either through the present emergency powers or through an increase in physical domination. That the present policy has reached its limits is suggested by the fact that, after a period in which the regime appeared to be unable to offer anything new, reform initiatives are once more coming to the fore.

A REFORMIST SOLUTION?

This is not to suggest that the regime is advancing a clearly defined, new package of reforms in advance of the elections due to take place in May 1987. The question I wish to pose relates to the likely consequences of the type of reforms which are currently under discussion. These are, firstly, proposals for the creation of a fourth house of Parliament for the representation of the African people linked in some way to the Bantustans and, secondly, a proliferation of regional arrangements along the lines proposed by the Natal/ Kwazulu Ndaba.

It is clear that neither of these reforms meets the demands of the national liberation movement. The first leaves power in the hands of the white Parliament and, more specifically, the State President and the President's Council, the second leaves unchanged white control of state power at the national level. As in the case of previous reforms, the issue once again arises as to the political space which such reforms will make available to the mass democratic movement to develop its organisational strengths. For, whether the state of emergency remains in place or not, (legislation has now been passed giving the regime emergency-type powers without the necessity of declaring an emergency), such reforms, if they are to function as reforms at all, will necessarily serve to constrain the operation of the regime's repressive apparatuses.

Herein lies the dilemma facing the regime. Shut off from the possibility of a coercive solution it can only hope to stabilise the political situation through reforms which will win support from important constituencies among black people. However, given the configuration of white interests, notwithstanding the reformist postures of corporate capital and others, it can offer only extremely limited reforms. Since those reforms are concerned with black representation and not merely with redistribution by way of education, wages, housing and so forth, they necessarily provide the political conditions for a resurgence of the mass democratic movement.

CONCLUSION

If, however, the regime is unable to solve the political crisis through either repression or limited reforms or, indeed, a combination of both, it does not necessarily follow that the balance will automatically be weighted in favour of the national liberation movement to such an extent that it will be able to dislodge the present government or any other regime committed to white supremacy. Even if the regime cannot tilt the balance in its own favour, a situation of unstable equilibrium may be maintained over a long period of time.

To break that equilibrium, would require an all round weakening of the South African state and, in particular, of its military and security forces. This would require an escalation of the armed struggle inside the country involving the shift from 'armed propaganda' to 'people's war' to which the ANC is committed. The South African army is probably too strong to be defeated in a direct military confrontation by a guerilla force. That, however, does not at once arise in the South African situation for the mass insurrectionary political movement is the principal agent of the struggle for national liberation. The state's capacity to defeat or control that movement would, however, be seriously impeded if it were substantially engaged by guerilla actions on a large and dispersed scale.

The South African revolutionary struggle stands at the crossroads: the ability of the mass democratic organisations to withstand the full repressive onslaught of the state is being put to the test, but the overthrow of the regime and the apartheid system will depend upon escalation of the armed struggle and its combination with the insurrectionary movement. That conjuncture remains to be achieved by the national liberation movement.

# Notes

CHAPTER 1

1. See, for example, Bunting, 1964, p. 305.
   There is also other writing which actually attempts to analyse the specificity of historical changes but which, at the same time, generalises South African history in a manner which departs from the actual analysis offered and appears to suggest the continuity there which is here being criticised. See, for example, Slovo 1976 and Legassick 1972, p. 31.
2. It is not necessary to cite references here for virtually all accounts of black education in South Africa which focus on descriptive accounts of the advantages of white and the glaring deficiencies in black education assume that the demonstration of the continuation of inequality exhausts the subject. Typical are the empirically very rich accounts of the South African Institute of Race Relations Annual Survey.
3. See, for example, Legassick 1974; Wolpe 1972; Davies 1979; Slovo 1976.
4. See the meaning given to these terms in the Introduction.
5. For discussions see the articles collected in Rex and Mason 1986; Kuper and Smith 1969; Miles 1982; Unesco 1980.
6. For example, Marquard 1957; Carter et al, 1967.
7. See, for example, Von Onselen 1982.
8. Wolpe 1980, 1984.

CHAPTER 2

1. See Poulantzas 1973, 1974, 1978.
2. Although M. O'Dowd, who was a leading proponent of this approach (see 1974), was and is a high ranking executive in the Anglo-American Corporation.
3. The view that economic development would eradicate racial domination has, of course, also been espoused by foreign corporations and foreign governments, notably Britain and the U.S. Their response to declining profits and political instability in the present

situation has been to continue with the old argument or to withdraw their capital.

4. See South African Communist Party 1962; ANC 1977.

5. See, for example, Clarke 1978.

6. It is of interest that the state has in the present period begun to recruit unemployed Africans, largely from the bantustans, to form vigilante groups to work with the police in urban townships. They are uniformed and armed and are notorious for their brutality towards members of the democratic organisations.

7. Bunting's book deals primarily with the 1960s.

CHAPTER 3

1. See among other texts: Poulantzas 1974, Gramsci 1971.

2. The struggles over education in black schools and universities is a dramatic case in point. See, for example, Brooks and Brickhill 1980, Hirson 1979.

CHAPTER 4

1. See section 3 of Chapter 1.

2. The acknowledgement by law enforcement agencies of the authority of the courts would be easy to illustrate by numerous examples, but one will suffice. In March 1960, the Supreme Court declared the proclamation of a state of emergency to be defective on a technical ground to do with proof of publication. The court granted a writ of habeas corpus and ordered a number of detainees to be released. The police manipulated the situation by releasing the detainees from the cells but used various reasons for keeping them in the police charge office until the regulations were properly published some hours later. Nonetheless, they were not prepared to actually imprison the detainees in defiance of the court order.

3. These changes followed the Wiehahn and Riekert Commissions.

CHAPTER 5

1. The Congress Alliance was formed in the 1950s. It co-ordinated the political work, particularly in the organisation of mass campaigns, of the South African Congress, the Coloured People's Organisation, the South African Congress of Democrats and the South African Congress of Trade Unions and the ANC.

2. See O'Meara 1985.
3. See Innes 1983.
4. Nolutshungu 1984.
5. There are some exceptions to this the most important being in Kwandebele where an organised struggle against the acceptance of 'independent' status for the bantustan succeeded.
6. There is, of course, a voluminous literature on the theory of the state. Some of this literature is listed and discussed in Wolpe 1980, particularly as it was developed in relation to South Africa. See also Chapter 2.
7. See for example the report of the December 1985 National Education Crisis Conference which had difficulty in meeting because of Inkatha strong arm tactics.
8. For an elaboration of the economistic politics of NAFCOC and the petite bourgeoisie generally see Jordan 1984; Wolpe 1977.
9. Jordan 1985.

# Bibliography

Adam, H. 1971, *Modernizing Racial Domination* (Berkeley: University of California Press)

Adam, H. and H. Giliomee, 1979, *Ethnic Power Mobilized* (Yale)

Adam, H. and K. Moodley, 1986, *South Africa Without Apartheid* (Berkeley: University of California Press)

African National Congress, 1977, *ANC Speaks*

—(n.d.) *Colonialism of a Special Type* (ANC, Lusaka)

—1987, *Advance to People's Power* (Statement on 75th Anniversary of the ANC)

African National Congress and Inyandza National Movement 1986, *Joint Communique* following Meeting, Lusaka 1–3 March.

Arnold, M. 1978, *The Testimony of Steve Biko* (Temple Smith)

Biko, S. 1972, White Racism and Black Consciousness, in H. Van der Merwe and D. Welsh (Eds), *Student Perspectives on South Africa* (David Philip)

Brooks, A. and J. Brickhill, 1980, *Whirlwind Before the Storm* (IDAF)

Budlender, D. 1984, Technological Change and Labour on 'White' Farms, in *South African Review* 2 (Ravan Press)

Bunting, B. 1964, *The Rise of the South African Reich* (Penguin)

Burawoy, M. 1985, *The Politics of Production* (Verso Books)

Cachalia, F. 1983, The State, Crisis and Restructuring: 1970–80, in *African Perspectives*; 23

Carter, G.M., T. Karis and N.M. Stultz 1967, *South Africa's Transkei: The Politics of Domestic Colonialism* (Heinemann)

Cawthra, G. 1986, *Brutal Force: The Apartheid War Machine* (IDAF)

Charton, N. (Ed) 1980, *Ciskei: Economics and Politics of Dependence in a South African Homeland.* (Croom Helm)

Clarke, S. 1978, Capital, Fractions of Capital and the State: 'Neo-Marxist' Analysis of the South African State, *Capital and Class*, 5

Central Statistical Services 1982, *South African Statistics* (Government Printer)

Cohen, R. 1986, *Endgame in South Africa?* (James Currey, Unesco)

Collinge, J. 1986, The United Democratic Front, *South African Review* (Ravan Press)

Crankshaw, O. 1985, Marxist Theories of Class and the Emerging African 'Middle Class' in South Africa (mimeo; paper presented to the Association of Sociology in South Africa Conference)

Davies, R. 1979, *Capital, State and White Labour in South Africa, 1900–1960* (Harvester Press)

Davies, R., D. O'Meara and S. Dhlamini 1984, *The Struggle for South Africa*, 2 Volumes. (Zed Press)

Davis, D. and Bob Fine 1985, Political Strategies and the Law: Some Historical Observations, *Journal of Southern African Studies*, 12, 1

Davis, R., D. Kaplan, M. Morris and D. O'Meara 1976, Class Struggles and the Periodization of the South African State, *Review of African Political Economy*, 7

de Klerk, M. 1984, Technological Change and Farm Labour: A Case Study of Maize Farming in the Western Transvaal, (ed) SARS *South African Review*, 2 (Ravan Press)

Dunbar, T. Moodie, 1975, *The Rise of Afrikanerdom* (University of California Press)

Fine, B. 1984, *Democracy and the Rule of Law*, (Macmillan)

Frankel, P.H. 1984, *Pretoria's Praetorians*, (Cambridge University Press)

Gramsci, A. 1971, *Selection from the Prison Notebooks* (Lawrence and Wishart)

Greenberg, S. 1980, *Race and State in Capitalist Development* (Yale University Press)

Hall, S. 1980, See UNESCO

Hayson, N. 1983, *Ruling with the Whip: Report on the Violation of Human Rights in the Ciskei* (CIIR)

—1986, *Apartheid Private Army: The Rise of Right Wing Vigilantes in South Africa* (CIIR)

Hendler, P., A, Mabin and S. Parnell 1986, Rethinking Housing Questions in South Africa, in *South African Review*, 3 (Ravan Press)

Hirson, B. 1979, *Year of Fire, Year of Ash*, (Zed Press)

Horwitz, R. 1967, *The Political Economy of South Africa* (Weidenfeld and Nicolson)

Hudson, Peter A. 1986, The Freedom Charter and Socialist Strategy in South Africa, *Politikon*, 13, 1

Hughes, H. and J. Grest 1983, The Local State, in *South African Review*, 1 (Ravan Press)

Hyslop, J. 1986 State Education Policy and the Social Reproduction of the Urban African Working Class: 1955–1976 (unpublished mimeo)

Innes, D 1983, Monopoly Capitalism in South Africa, *South African Review*, (Ravan Press)

International Defence and Aid Fund 1981, South Africa: Entrenchment of White Domination (Briefing Paper 3)

—1985, Reshaping the Constitution of Apartheid (Briefing Paper 16)

Jaffe, G. 1986, Beyond the Cannon of Mamlodi, *Work in Progress*, 41

Jessop, B. 1982, *The Capitalist State* (Martin Robertson)

Jordan, Z. Pallo 1983, Socialist Transformation and the Freedom Charter. Paper prepared on behalf of the ANC Research Unit for the *Southern African Universities Social Science Conference*, Harare, September, 1983

—*The African Petty Bougeoisie: A Force for Change or for the Status Quo?* (ANC Research Unit, Lusaka)

Kaplan, D. 1980, The South African State: the Origins of a Racially Exclusive Democracy, *Insurgent Socialist*, X, 2

Keenan, J. 1984, Agribusiness and the Bantustans, *South African Review*, 2 (Ravan Press)

Kuper, L. and M.G. Smith (Eds), 1971, *Pluralism in Africa* (University of California Press)

Legassick, M. 1974, South Africa: Capital Accumulation and Violence, *Economy and Society*, 3, 3

—1975, South Africa: Forced Labour, Industrialization and Racial Differentiation in R. Harris, *The Political Economy of Africa* (John Wiley & Son)

Lipton, M. 1985, *Capitalism and Apartheid* (Gower/Maurice Temple Smith)

Marquard, L. 1957, *South Africa's Colonial Policy* (South African Institute of Race Relations)

Marx, K. 1859, Introduction to *A Contribution to the Critique of Political Economy* (Progress Publishers, 1976)

Mbeki, G. 1964, *South Africa: The Peasants' Revolt* (Penguin Books)

Miles, R. 1982, *Racism and Migrant Labour* (Routledge and Kegan Paul)

Nattrass, J. 1981, *The South African Economy: Its Growth and Change* (Oxford University Press)

NECC 1986, South Africa in Crisis: Report on The Second National Education Conference, South Africa, 29–30 March, 1986 (CIIR)

Nolutshungu, S. 1982, *Changing South Africa: Political Considerations* (Manchester University Press)

Nyawuza 1985, New 'Marxist' Tendencies and the Battle For Ideas in South Africa, *The African Communist*, 103, 4th Quarter

O'Dowd, M.C. 1978, The Stages of Economic Growth and the Future of South Africa in L. Schlemmer and E. Webster, *Change, Reform and Economic Growth in South Africa* (Ravan Press)

O'Meara, D. 1982, Muldergate and the Politics of Afrikaner Nationalism, *Work in Progress*, 22

—1983, *Volkskapitalisme* (Cambridge University Press)

Pityana, B. 1972, Power and Social Change in South Africa, in H.W. van der Merwe and D. Welsh (Eds.), *Student Perspectives on South Africa* (David Philip)

Platsky, L. and C. Walker 1985, *The Surplus People: Forced Removals in South Africa* (Ravan Press)

Poulantzas, 1973, *Political Power and Social Classes* (New Left Books)

—(1974) *Classes in Contemporary Capitalism* (New Left Books)

—1979, *State Power and Socialism* (New Left Books)

Rex, J. and D. Mason (Eds), 1986, *Theories of Race and Ethnic Relations* (Cambridge University Press)

Riekert Report, 1979, *Report of the Commission of Enquiry into Legislation Affecting the Utilisation of Manpower,* RP/32

Rogers, B. 1980, *Divide and Rule: South Africa's Bantustans* (IDAF)

Rostow, W. 1960, *The Stages of Development* (Cambridge University Press)

Sachs, A. 1973, *Justice in South Africa* (Heinemann)

Sarkinsky, M. 1986, The State, White Capital and the Urban African Bourgeoisie in South Africa: Class Interests and Political Strategies (ROAPE Conference, Liverpool University, September, mimeo)

Saul, John S. and Stephen Gelb, 1986, *The Crisis in South Africa* (Zed Press)

Saul, John S. 1986, Class, Race and the Future of Socialism in South Africa. Paper presented to a conference on *The Southern African Economy After Apartheid,* Centre For Southern African Studies, University of York, 29th September – 2nd October, 1986

Simons, H.J. and R. 1969, *Class and Colour in South Africa 1850–1950* (Penguin)

Simson, H. 1980, *The Social Origins of Afrikaner Fascism and Its Apartheid Policy,* Uppsala Studies in Economic History, 21 (Stockholm: Almquist & Wiksell International)

—1983, Is the Apartheid State a Fascist State? A Framework for Analysis, *South African Studies, Retrospect and Prospect* (University of Edinburgh)

Slovo, J. 1976, South Africa – No Middle Road in B. Davidson, J. Slovo and A.R. Wilkinson, *Southern Africa: the New Politics of Revolution,* (Penguin Books)

—1981, Speech Delivered on the Occasion of the 60th Anniversary of the South African Communist Party (Maputo, mimeo)

—1986, SACP – One of the Great Pillars of Our Revolution. *African Communist,* 107, 4th Quarter

South African Communist Party, 1962, *The Road to South African Freedom Programme of the South African Communist Party* (Inkululeko Press)

South African Communist Party, 1981, *South African Communists Speak* (Inkululeko Publications)

Southall, R. 1982, *South Africa's Transkei: The Political Economy of an 'Independent' Bantustan* (Heinemann)

Streek, B. and R. Wicksteed, 1981, *Render unto Kaiser: A Transkei Dossier* (Ravan Press)

South African Institute of Race Relations, 1983, *Survey of Race Relations in South Africa*

Suttner, Raymond, 1984, The Freedom Charter – The People's Charter in the 1980s, *The Twenty-Sixth T.B. Davie Memorial Lecture,* Delivered in the University of Cape Town, September 26, 1984

UNESCO, 1980 *Sociological Theories: Race and Colonialism* (Unesco)

Unterhalter, E. (forthcoming), *Removals in Apartheid South Africa,* (IDAF)

Van Onselen, C. 1982, *Studies in the Social and Economic History of the Witwatersrand 1886–1914. Vol. 1 New Babylon, Vol. 2 New Nineveh* (Longmans)

Wiehahn Report, 1979, *Report of the Commission of Enquiry into Labour Legislation,* RP47

Wolpe, H. 1978, The Changing Class Structure of South Africa: The African Petit-Bourgeoisie, in P. Zarembka (Eds), *Research in Political Economy* (IAP)

—1978, A Comment on 'The Poverty of Neo-Marxism', in *Journal of Southern African Studies,* 4, 2

—1980, Towards an Analysis of the South African State, *The International Journal for the Sociology of Law.* 8

—1983, The Analysis of the South African State – A Critique of the Concept of South African Fascism, in *South African Studies Retrospect and Prospect* (Edited M. Fransman) (University of Edinburgh)

—1984, Strategic Issues in the South African National Liberation Struggle in *Review,* 8, Fall

—1985, Strategies Towards the Law in South Africa: Analytical Considerations, in *Journal of Southern African Studies,* V 12

—1986 Class Concepts, Class Struggle and Race, in John Rex & D. Mason (Ed.), op. cit.

—1987, National and Class Struggle in South Africa, in *Africa's Crisis* (Institute for African Alternatives)

Also in the Unesco Series
**Apartheid and Society**

Peter H. Katjavivi

**NAMIBIA: A HISTORY OF RESISTANCE**

Namibia is the last African colony still fighting for independence from European rule. It offers a unique form of domination – occupation by South Africa and the infliction of apartheid.

Dr Katjavivi – himself a Namibian – traces the stages in the history of resistance:

**the Herero, Nama and other resistance to German conquest**
**the South African take-over under the League of Nations Mandate**
**land, labour and community-based resistance from 1920 to 1960**
**the emergence of Nationalist organisations**
**appeals to the United Nations and the International Court of Justice**
**the launching of SWAPO's armed struggle**
**nationalist responses to South Africa's Bantustan policy**
**the continuing war and the involvement of Angola**

The UN General Assembly terminated the League of Nations Mandate on 27 October 1967. We have now entered the third decade of South Africa's illegal occupation.

Peter Katjavivi has been a leading activist in the Namibian Nationalist Movement SWAPO. In 1986 he completed his doctoral thesis at St Antony's College Oxford on *The Rise of Nationalism in Namibia and its International Dimensions*. He is thus particularly well qualified to place the liberation war in the context of the international diplomatic battle to try and get South Africa to withdraw peacefully; he shows how the Western Contact Group have been frustrated by South Africa's continual changes of direction; and he traces the refusal of South Africa to allow free democratic elections under United Nations supervision. He analyses how perceived South African and US strategic interests have combined to defer a negotiated independence settlement.

**Is there an end to the continued exploitation of the mineral wealth of the country and its position as a buffer state between black Africa and apartheid in South Africa?**

Also in the Unesco Series
**Apartheid and Society**

Robin Cohen

**ENDGAME IN SOUTH AFRICA?**

- **the white monopoly of political power**
- **the attempt to make race coincide with space**
- **the regulation of the labour supply**
- **the maintenance of social control**

These are the four pillars of apartheid. If white political power is dislodged will the three other pillars now actually crumble?

**Apartheid is dying but will it lie down?**

Some Press Opinions

'As might be expected from one of the leading figures in his field, Cohen's short book is ably written, refreshingly free of conceptual clutter, authoritative in its deployment of comparative insights, and lucid in exposition. It forms at the same time a short textbook case-study in applied social theory and an analysis of the potential for radical change in the central ideological and political structures oif the apartheid order.' Richard Moorsom in *Third World Quarterly*.

'... a blend of analysis and prediction about what the future might bring ... Cohen sees South Africa as in "the beginnings of a new long-term unstable equilibrium, such as that obtaining in Northern Ireland or Lebanon", which is likely to be characterised by "unfocussed (and more directed) violence, urban disorder, mass struggle, state brutality and economic crisis" ... A brief review can do scant justice ... draws fruitfully on the work by human geographers on the relationship between spatial relations. His sophisticated analysis of the role of ideology is offered with wit and insight.' J.E. Spence, Professor of Politics, University of Leicester in *The Times Literary Supplement*.

'... a model for really long-term and searching academic analysis ...' Terence Ranger, Professor of Race Relations, University of Oxford.

'... its crisp text and lack of jargon make it a useful contribution to student reading lists.' Paul B. Rich in *African Affairs*

*Robin Cohen* is Director of the Centre for Research in Ethnic Relations and Professor of Sociology at the University of Warwick. He was previously Professor of Sociology at the University of the West Indies, Trinidad. His publications include *Labour and Politics in Nigeria* (1974, new ed. 1982) and *The New Helots: Migrants in the International Division of Labour* (1986).